LANCHESTER LIBRARY

3 8001 00581 4185

D1492910

Accounting Education:
Charting the Course
through a Perilous Future

LANCHESTER LIBRARY, Coventry University
Gosford Street, Coventry CVI 5DD Telephone 024 7688 7555

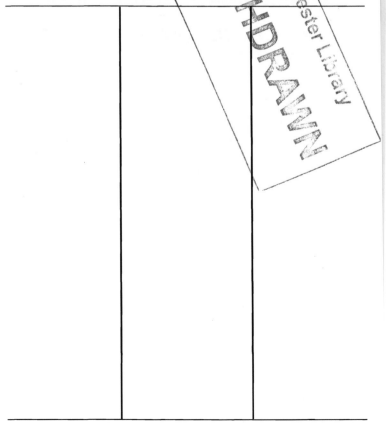

This book is due to be returned not later than the date and
time stamped above. Fines are charged on overdue books

Accounting Education:
Charting the Course
through a Perilous Future

By

W. Steve Albrecht, Brigham Young University
Robert J. Sack, University of Virginia

A JOINT PROJECT OF:
American Accounting Association
American Institute of Certified Public Accountants
Institute of Management Accountants
Arthur Andersen • Deloitte & Touche • Ernst & Young
KPMG • PricewaterhouseCoopers

August 2000

© 2000 by the American Accounting Association.
All rights reserved.

ISBN 0-86539-088-6
Printed in the United States of America

American Accounting Association
5717 Bessie Drive
Sarasota, FL 34233

Table of Contents

Foreword

All of us, as accounting educators, have been warned many times that accounting education must change if it is to be relevant and add value to our students and the community. Some educators have heard these warnings and have made significant changes to their programs and curricula. However, there is considerable evidence suggesting that changes to accounting education have not been pervasive or substantive enough. We are experiencing decreases in student enrollments and we still hear continued criticisms of our educational programs. Now, we are hearing disturbing statements by practicing accountants and even educators—statements that if they were completing their education over again, they would major in something other than accounting. These are serious problems.

We believe the critics are right. The time for change "just to be better" is past. We must now transform our educational programs merely to survive. We are threatened by changes in the marketplace, some of which are beyond our control. Nonetheless, there are a number of things we can do to shape our future, and we dare not delay. The time for action is now.

Four major groups that have a desire to improve accounting education joined together to sponsor this study—the Institute of Management Accountants (IMA), the American Institute of Certified Public Accountants (AICPA), the American Accounting Association (AAA), and the Big 5 professional service firms. We are deeply indebted to them for their support of this project. Their charge to us was to "write a high-level thought piece, supported by evidence where possible, about the future of accounting education."

Each of these organizations provided two members of the "Sponsors Task Force." The Task Force provided continued guidance throughout the project. At those times when we needed strategic guidance, they worked closely with us. We are very grateful for the helpful comments and direction provided by Bud Kulesza and Keith Russell of the IMA, Karen Pincus and Bea Sanders of the AICPA, Jan Williams and Michael Diamond of the AAA, and Brent Inman and Ellen Glazerman of the Big 5. We also appreciate those who were kind enough to permit personal interviews and those who participated in our focus groups. Without their participation, this report would not have been possible. Finally, we appreciate the help of Danny R. Olsen and Steven A. Wygant of the Brigham Young University Assessment Office who assisted with data analysis.

We make bold statements about accounting education in this report. Where possible, we have supported these statements with empirical evidence. You may disagree with some of our statements. We anxiously hope you will agree with our overall conclusion—that the accounting education environment cries out for action.

—W. Steve Albrecht and Robert J. Sack

About the Authors

W. Steve Albrecht, Ph.D., CPA, CIA, and CFE, is the Arthur Andersen LLP Alumni Professor of Accounting and Associate Dean of the Marriott School of Management at Brigham Young University. He previously taught at the University of Illinois and was a visiting professor at Stanford University. He has been the President of the American Accounting Association, Accounting Programs Leadership Group, Association of Certified Fraud Examiners and is currently President-elect of Beta Alpha Psi. He has also served on the Board of Regents of the Institute of Internal Auditors, the Board of Directors of the Utah Association of CPAs and is currently an at-large member of the AICPA Council. He has consulted with numerous corporations in the area of fraud prevention, detection, and investigation and has been an expert witness in many large fraud cases. He is the author of 16 books and monographs and over 80 journal articles.

Robert J. Sack, CPA, is an emeritus Professor of Business Administration at the Darden Graduate School of Business Administration, University of Virginia. He recently served as the Vice President of Publications for the American Accounting Association. He was a partner at Touche Ross & Co. (now Deloitte & Touche), serving as a line partner, as Director of Professional Standards for Touche Ross International, and as Director of Audit Practice for the U.S. firm. In his early days with Touche Ross, he was a member of the initial team of case writers and discussion leaders for the Trueblood Seminars Program. Before joining the Darden faculty, he served as the Chief Accountant in the Enforcement Division of the Securities and Exchange Commission. He is a member of the AAA, the IMA, the AICPA, and the Ohio and Virginia State CPA Societies.

About the Sponsoring Organizations

This study had four sponsors: the American Institute of Certified Public Accountants (AICPA), the Institute of Management Accountants (IMA), the American Accounting Association (AAA), and the Big 5 professional service firms (Arthur Andersen, Deloitte & Touche, Ernst & Young, KPMG, and PricewaterhouseCoopers). Each of these sponsors provided financial support, survey and focus group access to its members, and two task force members who provided guidance throughout the study.

About the Sponsors Task Force Members

Michael A. Diamond (AAA Representative), Ph.D., CPA, is Executive Vice Provost of the University of Southern California. He is immediate Past-President of the AAA and was formerly Director of Education for the AAA. He previously served as President of the Accounting Program Leaders Group and as chair of several AAA committees. At USC, he has served as Dean of the Leventhal School of Accounting, Director of the school's SEC and Financial Reporting Institute, and Vice Provost for Planning and Budget. Professor Diamond has written two accounting textbooks and has published articles in several accounting journals. Prior to becoming Dean at USC, Professor Diamond taught at California State University, Los Angeles and was a Visiting Professor at the University of California at Berkeley and the University of California, Los Angeles. He received the California Society of CPAs Faculty Excellence Award in 1993. He has consulted with the Strategic Planning Partnership, an initiative of the Ernst & Young Foundation, which has assisted many business schools and other academic organizations in strategic-planning and change-management processes.

Ellen Glazerman (Big 5 Representative) is the Director of the Ernst & Young Foundation and the National Director of Campus Recruiting for Ernst & Young LLP. She joined Ernst & Young LLP in May 1993 as the Director of the Ernst & Young Foundation. The Ernst & Young Foundation makes gifts to higher education in support of the firm's people-acquisition strategies. Ms. Glazerman is currently serving as Vice President of the American Accounting Association and is a member of the Board of Directors of the Accounting Programs Leadership Group. Prior to joining Ernst & Young, Ms. Glazerman spent nine years as a development officer for several universities, including St. Lawrence University, Colorado School of Mines and the University of Southern California. She has a B.A. from Wesleyan University and an M.B.A. from the University of Southern California.

Brent C. Inman (Big 5 Representative), a partner with PricewaterhouseCoopers, is the firm's leader for human resources development in the United States. His responsibilities include recruiting, compensation, work-life effectiveness, human-resource policy development, and the PricewaterhouseCoopers Foundation. Mr. Inman is Chairman of the Global Recruitment Group that is responsible for developing global recruitment strategies. Mr. Inman has been very active in professional organizations, including service as Vice President of the American Accounting Association, Board of Directors member of Accounting Programs Leadership Group and American Taxation Association, Vice Chairman of the Auditing Section of the AAA, and member of accounting accreditation and peer-review committees of the American Assembly of Collegiate Schools of Business (AACSB) and Beta Alpha Psi's task force on Future Goals and Directions of Beta Alpha Psi. In addition, he co-authored "Square Pegs in Round Holes: Are Accounting Students Well-Suited in Today's Accounting Profession" published in *Issues in Accounting Education*. Mr. Inman received his Bachelor's degree from Bradley University.

C. S. "Bud" Kulesza (IMA Representative), CMA, CFM, is the Chairman of the Institute of Management Accountants (IMA). Mr. Kulesza earned an Associate degree in Accounting from Middlesex County Community College and his Bachelor's degree in Commerce from Rider University. He began his accounting career with Johnson & Johnson and, after five years, joined ITT. During his career with ITT, he has held a number of Senior Financial positions in ITT's manufacturing companies. His industry experience includes food processing, telecommunications, electronic components, and automotive parts with multinational responsibilities. He is currently with ITT Industries, White Plains, New York serving as an Executive Consultant after having served, most recently, as Senior Vice President Finance for ITT Automotive in Auburn Hills, Michigan. Mr. Kulesza is the key spokesperson for the IMA's Practice Analysis of Management Accounting. Mr. Kulesza is a member of the Financial Executives Institute, the American Accounting Association, and the AACSB Accounting Accreditation Committee.

About the Sponsors Task Force Members (Continued)

Karen V. Pincus (AICPA Representative), Ph.D., CPA, is Professor and Chair of the Accounting Department in the Sam M. Walton College of Business Administration at the University of Arkansas. She previously spent 12 years on the faculty of the School of Accounting at the University of Southern California. As part of USC's Year 2000 Curriculum Project, Professor Pincus developed Core Concepts of Accounting Information, an innovative introductory accounting course for undergraduate students. In 1992, she received the AAA's Innovation in Accounting Education Award for the course. Professor Pincus has published numerous articles on audit judgment, fraud detection, and accounting education. Professor Pincus has served as Vice President of the AAA, President of the Federation of Schools of Accountancy, Board of Directors of Accounting Programs Leadership Group, President of the Auditing Section of the AAA, and currently serves as Chair of the AICPA's Pre-certification Executive Education Committee (PcEEC).

Keith A. Russell (IMA Representative), Ph.D., CMA, is a Professor of Accounting, Finance, and Business policy at Southeast Missouri State University. He served as IMA's Distinguished Professor-in-Residence for 1998 and 1999. He currently serves on IMA's Strategic Planning Committee. Professor Russell has won numerous teaching awards. He has published several articles on accounting education and management accounting, and consistently publishes and presents at the national level. He works with the Chamber of Commerce and engages in consulting to maintain professional currency.

Bea Sanders (AICPA Representative) is the Director of academic and career development for the American Institute of Certified Public Accountants (AICPA). She is responsible for programs to enhance the quality of accounting education and attract talented students to become CPAs, and oversees the AICPA's workforce diversity initiatives. She is also Secretary of the AICPA Foundation, which supports programs to advance the profession and accounting education. Ms. Sanders is a member of the National Advisory Forum of Beta Alpha Psi and is a technical advisor on the IFAC Education Committee. She has served on committees of the American Accounting Association and the Federation of Schools of Accountancy, and was a member of the AACSB's Accounting Accreditation Visitation Committee.

Jan R. Williams (AAA Representative), Ph.D., CPA, is the Ernst & Young Professor and Acting Dean of the College of Business Administration at the University of Tennessee. He has been extensively involved in professional accounting activities with the American Accounting Association, AICPA, Tennessee Society of CPAs, and other organizations. He is the President of the AAA for 1999–2000. He currently serves on a task force of the AICPA that is redesigning the CPA examination to meet the changing needs of accounting practice for the 21st century. His primary teaching and research interests are corporate financial reporting. He is the author or co-author of five books and over 70 articles and other publications on issues of financial reporting and accounting education. He teaches regularly in the University of Tennessee's M.B.A. and Master of Accountancy programs.

CHAPTER 1

Why Accounting Education
May Not Survive in the Future

While we have been long-time supporters of accounting education, if we were creating a new business school today, we would not have separate undergraduate or graduate accounting programs. At least, we would not have accounting programs that are structured as they are today.

—*W. Steve Albrecht and Robert J. Sack*

You may consider this quote to be blasphemous, especially coming from two people who have been heavily involved in accounting education, accounting accreditation, and accounting education leadership, but that statement reflects our true feelings. It is motivated by our belief that accounting education today is plagued with many serious problems and our concern that if those problems are not seriously addressed and overcome, they will lead to the demise of accounting education. Consider the following facts:

- The number and quality of students electing to major in accounting is decreasing rapidly. Students are telling us by their choice of major that they do not perceive an accounting degree to be as valuable as it used to be or as valuable as other business degrees.
- Both practicing accountants and accounting educators, most of whom have accounting degrees, would not major in accounting if pursuing their education over again.
- Accounting leaders and practicing accountants are telling us that accounting education, as currently structured, is outdated, broken, and needs to be modified significantly.

These are serious problems that cannot be ignored. Think about them in terms of the following diagram.

Inputs	**Current Accounting Education Model**	**Outputs**
The number of students majoring in accounting is down	Accounting practitioners say our educational model is broken and obsolete	Those who have majored in accounting would choose a different major if doing it over again

Really, it cannot get much worse. If our inputs are down, our value-added is being questioned, and those who have matriculated through our programs tell us they would not do it again, then what is our future? It probably would be possible to coast along for a few more years, especially if the economy stays strong, without making significant changes. We would have to live with less qualified students and reduced resources. In our surveys of accounting program leaders, department chairs told us that the major criterion upon which their budgets and faculty allocations are based is "number of students enrolled." Because of continuously declining enrollments, if we do not take action, we are destined to live with decreasing budgets, decreasing faculty positions, and, possibly, elimination of our accounting programs. If that possibility does not scare you, it certainly scares us!

Previous Warnings

We are not the first to warn of serious problems in accounting education. The Institute of Management Accountants (IMA), in three previous studies,[1] stated that accounting education needed to change if it is to meet the future needs of accountants in industry. The American Institute of Certified Public Accountants (AICPA), in its recent Vision Report,[2] called for modified accounting education programs to meet the future needs of CPAs. Fourteen years ago, the American Accounting Association's (AAA) Committee on Future Structure, Content and Scope of Accounting Education (the Bedford Committee)[3] called for a much broader role for accounting education than that being filled by most universities today. Consider the following 14-year-old quote from the Bedford report:

> *There is little doubt that the current content of professional accounting education, which has remained substantially the same over the past 50 years, is generally inadequate for the future accounting professional. A growing gap exists between what accountants do and what accounting educators teach....Accountants who remain narrowly educated will find it more difficult to compete in an expanding profession....The Committee's analysis of accounting practice has indicated that accounting education as it is currently approached requires major adjustments between now and the year 2000.*

The Big 5 (then Big 8) professional service firms, in their 1989 *White Paper,*[4] advocated changes in accounting education and felt so strongly that change was needed that they contributed five million dollars to fund the Accounting Education Change Commission. That Commission, through several publications and the funding of innovation in accounting education programs at several schools, called for significant changes in accounting education.

These previous efforts were very well done and have given us sufficient warning that accounting education must change to meet future needs of students.

Except in a few schools, these warning signals—warnings about the future viability of accounting education—have largely gone unheeded. In too many respects, accounting education is being delivered the same way today as it was 20 or 30 years ago. Certainly, part of the inaction can be explained by the booming economy we have experienced during the past ten years. In this economy, the penalty of making a wrong educational choice or of experiencing an inferior accounting education has been minimized. In an environment where most of our graduates have gained immediate, full-time employment upon graduation, it has been hard for us to recognize that there are serious problems with accounting education. In too many ways, the strong economy has lulled us into inaction, even though the warnings have been loud and consistent.[5]

---

[1] The three IMA studies are *Counting More, Counting Less*, published in 1999; *The Practice Analysis of Management Accounting,* published in 1996; and *What Corporate America Wants in Entry-Level Accountants*, published in 1994.

[2] *CPA Vision Project: Focus on the Horizon*, published in 1998.

[3] The report entitled *Future Accounting Education: Preparing for the Expanding Profession*, was published in 1986.

[4] *Perspectives on Education for Success in the Accounting Profession*, Big 8 firms.

[5] We recognize the viewpoint expressed by many educators that the primary problem with accounting education today is the low salaries being offered to our graduates. Other educators blame our current problems on the 150-hour rule. It is probably true that our most immediate crises would be mitigated if salary offers were increased by 15 percent and the 150-hour rule could be put on hold. However, it seems very unlikely that starting salaries for our graduates will be increased without action on our part to make those graduates more valuable; it is also unlikely that the state regulatory structure will declare a hiatus on the 150-hour rule, regardless of what we do. More importantly, we believe that the fundamental weaknesses in accounting education—weaknesses in curricula and pedagogy—are the more direct threats to our survival. And of course, they are the threats we can influence most directly.

Now, instead of encouraging change in accounting education in order to stay current (as former studies did), our message is more urgent. We believe that because practice has changed so dramatically and because accounting education has not kept up, we have lost ground to other business majors, to corporate competitors, and to other types of educational programs. In too many ways, business and technology have passed us by and we must now change quickly just to survive. We cannot emphasize strongly enough that it is now survival we are talking about, not merely changing to be better. There can be no further delays without serious consequences.

The Purpose and Nature of This Study

Because of the perceived lack of response by accounting educators to previous calls for action, and because of the fear of negative consequences for accounting education, four major organizations[6]—the Institute of Management Accountants (IMA), the American Institute of Certified Public Accountants (AICPA), the American Accounting Association (AAA), and the Big 5 professional service firms—joined together to sponsor this study.[7] Their charge to us was to write a "high-level thought piece, backed by empirical evidence where possible, that would motivate serious change in accounting education." They are sponsoring this study because their leaders feel strongly that accounting education must change quickly to survive. This monograph is the result of our study and thinking.[8]

Is There No Hope for Accounting Education?

The good news is that, while the gap between education and practice has been widening, with quick and definitive action we can save accounting education. There are many things that accounting educators do better than anyone else. In addition, there are many professional opportunities for which we can prepare our graduates. However, we cannot save accounting education by continuing to do more of the same. In the following chapters, we will discuss in detail the accounting education problems identified above and provide suggested solutions that, if acted upon quickly, will not only preserve accounting education, but will also make it more viable than ever before. Where possible, we will provide as much evidence as possible to substantiate our conclusions. In some cases, however, what we say will be our opinions. You probably will not agree with everything we have written. You may have better ideas than we do about how to change accounting programs to make them successful. We expect significant discourse about the details of this report and our suggestions for action. Disagreement at that level means that you have read this report and thought seriously about the issues. However, please do not ignore or treat lightly the issues we have raised. We urge you to consider seriously the issues raised and the potential consequences of those issues for your accounting programs and for your students.

Outline of the Monograph

In the following chapters, we explain in more detail the issues raised above. In Chapter 2, we discuss changes in the business environment, and how those changes are affecting accounting

---

[6] Obviously, the Big 5 firms are not one organization—in fact, they are competitors. However, because they joined together to co-sponsor this research, in this monograph they will be considered one of the four funding "organizations."

[7] We appreciate the funding and support of these organizations in helping us conduct our studies and write this report. Each of the organizations provided two members of what became the "sponsors' task force" that provided valuable insight and suggestions. The members of the task force are acknowledged by name in the Foreword.

[8] In addition to providing our own thoughts, we have gathered empirical evidence and perceptions from as many sources as possible. In preparing to write this monograph, we interviewed many key leaders in accounting and business. We held focus group sessions with approximately 30 participants at each session in four major cities throughout the United States. We accessed several supply-and-demand studies currently being conducted by the AICPA and others. We conducted three surveys of our own—one of accounting practitioners, one of accounting educators, and one of accounting department chairs. In addition, we used previous studies by the IMA, AECC, AICPA, and AAA. The details of our methodology are explained in the Appendix.

education. In Chapter 3, we focus on the problem of declining enrollments in accounting programs, both in terms of quantity and quality of students. In Chapter 4, we discuss why practicing accountants, even those who possess accounting degrees, would choose not to major in accounting if pursuing their educational programs again. In Chapter 5, we discuss why critics believe the accounting educational models used by most schools are broken and why they provide less value than they used to. Finally, in Chapter 6, we make an appeal for a school-by-school strategic-planning effort and offer some suggestions as to the direction those strategic plans might take.

An Apology to Some Accounting Educators

In conducting our background studies and from personal knowledge, we are aware that some accounting programs, schools, and faculty have made significant and meaningful changes in recent years. We applaud those efforts. However, the evidence is clear that, while there have been significant changes by some, the changes have not been significant or pervasive enough. We, like you, would be disappointed if only a few accounting programs survived into the future. It is with the hope that we can enhance and create value for all accounting programs that we undertook this study and wrote this report.

CHAPTER 2

Changes in the Business Environment

In order to understand why the number of students choosing to major in accounting has decreased and why professionals with accounting degrees would not major in accounting again, it is necessary to understand changes that have been taking place in business and how these changes have impacted business and accounting education. For many years, business relied on accountants to prepare financial information for internal and external decision making, to audit the fairness of that information and to assist them in fulfilling their regulatory and tax-reporting requirements. Information was expensive and understanding how to prepare accurate financial reports required expertise that could only be developed through rigorous accounting education or relevant experience. Rarely did an individual or institutional investor have sufficient power to influence management or require that specific information be provided. Organizational threats came largely from a few domestic competitors. Because information preparation and dissemination was expensive, product life cycles and competitive advantages could be managed effectively and inefficiencies were not readily observable.

Drivers of Change

At least three major developments have occurred that have changed dramatically the business environment for which we prepare graduates. First, technology has been developed that has made information preparation and dissemination inexpensive. This technology has taken the form of low-cost, high-speed digital and cable video and data transmission, hardware that produces information quickly and easily, and the development of software that makes preparation, data, and communication tools available to individuals who previously did not have access to needed information. With these technology developments, time, space, and other temporal constraints to information have been reduced and, in many cases, eliminated.

A second major development that has significantly impacted business has been globalization. Faster methods of transportation, together with instantaneous information, have allowed the world to become one giant marketplace. Consumers can now buy products from foreign firms as easily as they can from a local store. Organizations such as General Motors have to worry not only about what Chrysler and Ford are doing, but also what Toyota, Volkswagen, and BMW are doing as well. In fact, Chrysler is not just "Chrysler" anymore. It is now a conglomeration of European, North American, and Asian manufacturers known as DaimlerChrysler. Instead of having only two major American competitors, General Motors and all other business organizations now have to compete with similar companies throughout the world. In addition, with the increased availability of inexpensive information, more is known about these competitors and about General Motors than ever before. If a General Motors product has deficiencies, for example, the world knows about and can act on those problems instantly.

A third major change is the concentration of power in certain market investors, primarily large mutual and pension funds. Mutual funds such as Fidelity and Vanguard, and pensions funds such as CALPERS, for example, now hold major stock positions in many companies. The influence of these major market players is so significant that, if they are displeased, corporate executives will find that their positions within the company are in jeopardy. Armed with easily available and inexpensive information about investees and their competitors, large institutional investors raise the competitive bar very high and shorten the periods over which success is measured.

Our focus group participants and interviewees understood well these changes, as expressed in the following quotes:

I believe that one of the most important changes (affecting accounting practice) that has taken place in my experience is the changed relationship between the company and its investors. There is an explosion of required disclosures, and a huge increase in the interest the investment community has in those disclosures. The pressure for those increased disclosures is coming from both the SEC and from investors. The smart analyst will ask questions about the basic financials, but now will also ask about the company's strategic focus. They want to know what a firm's EVA measure is as proof of the company's strategic focus. —Interviewee

Technology has been an enabler, allowing us to do accounting more efficiently and at a lower cost, but what is driving change is the whole global competition and the demand the customer has for more responsiveness and more efficiency. —Participant, New York Focus Group

We are moving into an age of instant gratification—that seems to be true whether it's children, clients, or whatever—they want instant gratification and you have to provide answers now! We not only have to provide answers, but the right answers. As companies change, they can't get information fast enough and if they can't get it from us, they will get it somewhere else. —Participant, Atlanta Focus Group

There are lots of new services that we never even thought about historically. People want information much faster than ever before—they want instant feedback and gratification. The world is much more global than it used to be. Technology has changed the way we work and the way we think about things. —Participant, Atlanta Focus Group

Results of These Change Drivers

While these change drivers have significantly impacted everything we do, including the way we live, they have had two dramatic impacts on business. First, they have eliminated the old model that assumed information is expensive. Today anyone, armed with the right software, can be an "accountant" and produce financial information. Second, they have dramatically increased the level of competition among organizations. Institutional investors want the best performance and they want it now. Global competitors often have different cost structures that can be exploited to render historically successful business models obsolete; and since information about all organizations is widely available, only organizations that are truly the best survive and remain successful.

There have been a number of business developments because of these changes. Some of the most obvious are:

- An increased pace of change in the business world
- Shorter product life cycles and shorter competitive advantages
- A requirement for better, quicker, and more decisive actions by management
- Emergence of new companies and new industries
- Emergence of new professional services
- Outsourcing of non-value-added, but necessary, services

- Increased uncertainty and the explicit recognition of risk
- Increasingly complex business transactions
- Restructuring of rewards with:
  - Elimination of or reduction in rewards for services replaced by technology
  - Unchanged rewards for traditional, but needed services
  - Increased rewards for services that help leverage technology and globalization and that assist in making better strategic decisions
- Changes in financial reporting and relationships with financial markets and major market players
- Increased regulatory activity
- Increased focus on customer satisfaction

Increased Pace of Change, Shorter Product Life Cycles and Competitive Advantages, and Quicker and More Decisive Actions

The first question we asked in our surveys was "How would you describe the rate of change in the accounting profession during each of the following five-year periods, using 1 as representing no change and 5 as representing dramatic change?" Responses were as follows:

Time Period	Degree of Change— Faculty Responses	Degree of Change— Practitioner Responses
The first half of the 1980s (1980–1984)	2.56	2.65
The second half of the 1980s (1984–1989)	3.07	2.96
The first half of the 1990s (1990–1994)	3.54	3.41
The second half of the 1990s (1994–1999)	4.20	4.02
The next five years (2000–2004)	4.47	4.29

One interviewee stated it this way: "On a scale of 1 to 5, the next five years will be a 50." The consistently increasing nature of the responses leaves little doubt about the perceptions of change in the future. The results of an increased pace of change are products that do not last as long, and competitive advantages that have shorter lives. The sense of urgency that permeates business today is overwhelming. Competitive advantage is a short-lived asset and its potential must be exploited quickly and fully. Paradoxically, the need to move quickly has reduced the time available for analysis, just when it has become more necessary than ever to have better information in order to squeeze the last penny of profit from a product or investment. As has always been true, these challenges are also opportunities. For those who can take advantage of globalization and technology, the future is bright. For those who cannot, the future is grim. Two interviewees see these changes this way:

The business cycle is substantially shorter, the life cycle of products is shorter. Microsoft will tell you that their products change completely over three years. Look at GM and their market share decline—look how quickly that happened. —Interviewee

Today, the product life cycles are much, much shorter than they were before. Technology, in addition to being an enabler, is fueling all this dynamic change that is rippling through our clients, which in turn impacts us and our people. —Participant, New York Focus Group

Emergence of New Companies, Services and Industries and the Elimination and Outsourcing of Non-Value-Added Services

Every day in the *Wall Street Journal* or other financial news outlets there is a story of a new IPO. Look at your own stock portfolio and see how many companies and industries in which you invest were not in existence a few years ago. Consider the following three facts:

First, consider the number of patents issued by the U.S. government. The first patent under the current patent numbering system was issued in July 1836. Since that time, the number of patents issued has increased every year but one with 1999 having the largest increase and being the highest at almost 600,000 patents. Products and services covered by these patents will change the way we work and live in the future. In fact, it is amazing to think that the power of the world's most powerful and biggest computer 40 years ago can now be contained in a little computer that fits in your pocket. And if experts' predictions are right, in 40 more years, the power of today's biggest and most powerful computers will also be contained in a small pocket-size computer.1

Second, consider how these new industries and services have affected job tenure. The length of time employees stay with the same firm has now decreased to where, in 1998, the median job tenure for workers 25 and older was 4.7 years. In future years, your typical job will average 5 years or less and you will constantly be on the lookout for your "next" job. The promise or thought of "lifetime employment" is a myth that very few Americans will experience or even want to experience. Americans are being "downsized," "right-sized," and cut from their jobs in record numbers. For example, even though the period 1993–97 were years of high corporate profits and a robust economy, over 2 and one-half million workers were "laid off" by companies in the U.S.2

Third, consider how the way we work and do business in the U.S. is changing. We have moved away from a manufacturing to a service- and information-based society. As an example, if you look at a recent list of Forbes *magazine's 400 richest Americans, three of the top 14 are associated with companies that did not even exist 10 years ago, including Price-Line.com, Amazon.com, and eBay.com. If you add Bill Gates, Paul Allen, and Steven Ballmer of Microsoft, Michael Dell of Dell Computers, and Lawrence Ellison of Oracle Corp., only three of the 11 richest Americans are not from technology companies (Warren Buffet of Berkshire Hathaway, S. Robson Walton of Wal-Mart, and John Kluge of Metromedia Co.) 3*

Think about some of the headlines you have read recently: "Major Company Outsources its Accounting and Payroll Functions," "Big 5 Firm Sells Consulting Practice and Takes it Public," and "dot.com Company Sold for Billions." Even CPA firms have transformed themselves from "accounting" to "professional service" firms, offering services not even imagined a few years ago. One of our Los Angeles focus group participants expressed these changes well:

*I can't speak for all the Big 5, but certainly for my firm I think we've tried very hard to redefine ourselves as a "professional services firm." If you look at our business card, if you look at any of our ads, anything, they will say, " professional services firm." And, I think that's probably pretty consistent, certainly throughout the Big 5. —*Participant, Los Angeles Focus Group

Discussing just how far accounting firms have moved away from traditional accounting, another focus group participant stated:

*About six months ago, I received the annual report of KPMG. And, as I was kind of skimming through, it struck me that the term "accounting" did not appear in their annual report. So, I took it as a challenge and I read the 40 pages only to see if the term "accounting" appears there and it appears twice. Once they said that the firm is supporting Beta Alpha Psi, an accounting students' organization, and the other time was a box that describes the firm and says that they do accounting services. —*Participant, Los Angeles Focus Group

Increased Uncertainty and Complexity and an Increased Awareness of Risk

The emergence of additional competitors, the high demands of institutional investors, the global marketplace, and the need to make quick decisions have increased the level of uncertainty and

---

[1]   http://www.uspto.gov/web/offices/ac/ido/oeip/taf/issuyear.htm.
[2]   http://www.bls.census.gov/cps/pub/tenure_0296.htm.
[3]   http://www.forbes.com/tool/toolbox/billnew/net98.asp?condition=25,99.

complexity in the business world. Trying to get a competitive edge and use every possible avenue to increase profits, corporations have entered into highly complex transactions. Consider the following two quotes, for example.

The complexity of transactions has changed dramatically in the 16 years I've been with my firm. I started out working on the Delta Airlines audit and have probably worked on it 14 out of 16 years with the firm. Now, if you read their financials and look at the types of transactions that have taken place at just one company, you see things such as securitizations, derivatives, and hedges of foreign exchange and commodity risks. —Participant, Atlanta Focus Group

Because we have all this technology in the business world, models are becoming much more complex. There are very complex transactions that get invented in business and businesses get invented around these things very quickly. Accounting has trouble keeping pace with what should be the right answers for these kinds of transactions and sometimes, by the time we figure them out, the transactions or business becomes obsolete. —Participant, New York Focus Group

This complexity and uncertainty has given rise to new types of professional services focusing on understanding risk. Although many people expect the demand for audit services to decrease because an audit is a "commodity that adds little future value," this increase in risk may create an even higher demand for audit-type services in the future. One focus group member stated the following about uncertainty and risk:

We have developed a whole new framework to help companies understand that risk is not always a negative thing. Risk can be explored to be something positive. As accountants, we're having to think not just what the accounting standards are and doing them well, but how companies can manage risk in a very positive way. Clients are just absolutely fascinated by how risk in and of itself has evolved. I personally thought that risk was like not being insured. But today, we are looking at risk in a lot of different ways. Think about what happened with Coca-Cola in Europe when they had to pull all the products off the shelf. That was a risk that the company had taken and could have avoided. So we help companies with that. We help companies manage their risk framework. —Participant, Atlanta Focus Group

Restructuring of Rewards and Increased Attractiveness of Other College Majors

As firms try to react to these forces of change, they have altered the amount they pay for different kinds of services. Related to services provided by accounting graduates, three major shifts have occurred:

- Pay for scorekeeping-type services that can now be performed by anyone using the right kind of software has decreased.
- Pay for traditional services that are purchased because they are necessary, such as audit and tax compliance work, is under increased competitive pressure and has stayed fairly constant.
- Pay for services that help companies leverage technology and globalization or make strategic decisions has increased dramatically.

Consider, for example, the salaries paid to undergraduate business students (as reported by NACE)[4] between 1990 to 1999 by certain types of employers.

Type of Employer	1990 Average Salary	1999 Average Salary	Percent Increase
Public and Private Accounting	$26,400	$34,500	31
Investment Banking and Corporate Finance	$29,100	$37,100	28
Financial/Treasury Analysis	$26,700	$36,100	35
Information Systems/Computer Science	$29,100	$41,400	42
Consulting	$28,700	$42,600	48

[4] The National Association of Colleges and Employers (NACE), Bethlehem, Pennsylvania.

From these data, it is not hard to see where premiums are being paid. Graduates who work with technology or help make strategic decisions are being paid the highest premiums. Salaries in public and private accounting are currently the lowest.

Changes in Financial Reporting and Increased Regulatory Activity

The combined forces of globalization, technology, and increased power among certain institutional investors has changed the relationship between listed companies and the market and the way those companies report information. The results of these changes have been:

- Decreased reliance on historical financial statements
- More one-on-one contact between listed companies and major market decision makers and analysts
- More disclosure of nonfinancial information
- Movement away from traditional financial statements to database-type reporting

The result of these changes is less need for historical financial statements. As one focus group participant stated:

> *The way things have changed is that our clients no longer need us to crunch numbers the way we used to because technology now does that for them. What, in the past, used to be our deliverable— the financial statement—is now coming 60 to 90 days after year-end. It loses a lot of its importance because our clients (and their investors) no longer care what happened 60 or 90 days ago; they're looking for something to affect the bottom line in the operations of the business today.*
> —Participant, New York Focus Group

As CPA firms have moved beyond their traditional roles, regulators have worried that their independence will be compromised. The result has been increased regulatory activity by the Securities and Exchange Commission and other regulatory bodies, and more uncertainty within the profession. The profession is in the midst of an extraordinary transition, and it is not clear where that transition is heading.

Increased Focus on Customer Satisfaction

With immediately available information and global competition, customers have more information than ever before to use in making purchase decisions. The result of this increased information and globalization is greater and more discriminating purchasing power and influence by customers and a shift in power from sellers to customers. Customers can now, more than ever before, dictate terms of purchase transactions, including price, delivery times, and product and service specifications. This increased customer focus extends beyond purchasing goods and services from other entities to increased power by users of accounting and other information within entities. Operations managers and other users can now dictate the kind of information they want, when they need it, and how it is to be reported to them.

Summary of Changes

The following diagram illustrates the drivers of change, results of these changes, and developments that have occurred because of the changes that have taken place.

The Three Key Drivers of Change in the Business Environment are:

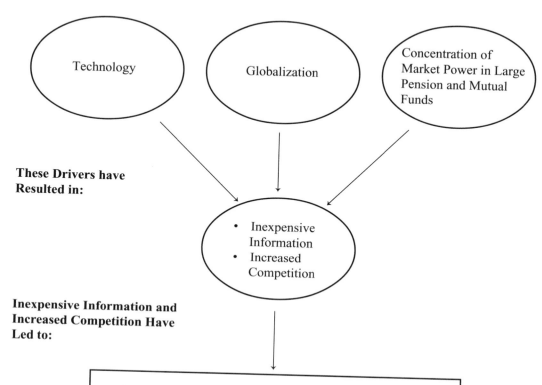

These Drivers have Resulted in:

Inexpensive Information and Increased Competition Have Led to:

- An increased pace of change in the business world
- Shorter product life cycles and shorter competitive advantages
- A requirement for better, quicker, and more decisive actions by management
- Emergence of new companies and new industries
- Emergence of new professional services
- Outsourcing of non-value added, but necessary, services
- Increased uncertainty and the explicit recognition of risk
- Increasingly complex business transactions
- Restructuring of rewards with:
  – Elimination of or reduction in rewards for services replaced by technology
  – Unchanged rewards for traditional, but needed services
  – Increased rewards for services that help leverage technology and globalization and that assist in making better strategic decisions
- Changes in financial reporting and relationships with financial markets and major market players
- Increased regulatory activity
- Increased focus on customer satisfaction

Reactions to These Changes by Accounting Associations and Professionals

Everyone agrees that change in business is occurring rapidly. The real question is whether accounting organizations, professionals, and educators are recognizing the changes and adapting quickly enough to the new environment. Consider how four accounting-related groups have reacted: (1) public practice, excluding the Big 5, (2) industry, (3) the Big 5 firms, and (4) education.

If we think of public accounting as being represented by the AICPA and smaller public accounting firms, how have they responded? The AICPA has recently undertaken a very comprehensive Vision project to identify new values, services, competencies, and issues it must deal with. It is redesigning and computerizing the CPA exam, developing new technology-related services, heading up a new global, broader-based professional certification program (XYZ certification), developing several specialty certifications, and is one of the major players in developing a new, consistent reporting format using XML programming language (XBRL.) The AICPA is scrambling to make changes that will keep its members successful and maintain its status as the preeminent nonprofit organization of practicing "accounting" professionals. Non-Big 5 CPA firms have reorganized and refocused the types of services they offer. Instead of performing mostly tax, audit, and write-up services, they have developed expertise in personal financial planning, fraud auditing, and business advising.

The Big 5 firms, more than any other group, have transformed themselves into completely different kinds of entities. No longer driven by audit and tax services, they have expanded the types of services they offer, the types of students and experienced hires they recruit, and no longer even refer to themselves as public accounting firms.[5] Because of regulatory pressure and other reasons, they have even broken apart into separate entities. They are paying premiums to students and employees who can provide services to clients that allow those clients to leverage technology and take advantage of globalization opportunities.

If we think of industry as being represented by the IMA and "accountants" working in organizations, how have they responded? The IMA has changed the name of its journal from *Management Accounting* to *Strategic Finance*. It no longer refers to its members as "management accountants" but instead as "finance professionals." It has added a new, international CMA/CFM certification and has initiated several major studies to understand what environmental changes mean for its members and, like the AICPA, is scrambling to find new services that will keep its members successful. Finance professionals (accountants) working inside companies have transformed themselves from scorekeepers working in isolated departments to trusted business professionals making decisions together with management.

So, what about accounting education? How have we responded to these changes? If we think of education as being represented by the AAA, individual school programs, and faculty members, what have we done? Like the AICPA and IMA, the AAA is scrambling to add services that will add value to its members. It has started a benchmarking program to help schools understand the kinds of changes being made at other schools. It has worked hard on electronic publication issues to take advantage of new publishing opportunities and not lose its valuable stream of publication revenues. It has placed significant emphasis on faculty development, hiring a full-time faculty development director to assist schools as they try to keep their faculty current. Members of the AAA have responded in different ways. At the institutional level, some schools have made significant changes, while others have been slow to change. Some faculty have engaged in aggressive faculty development and have worked hard to stay current while others have not.

---

[5] During the period 1993–1999, revenue from consulting services grew at a compound annual rate of 27 percent, tax revenue grew at 13 percent, and audit and assurance services revenue grew by 9 percent. In 1993, the Big 5 firms' accounting and auditing services averaged 51 percent of total fees; tax services were 22 percent; and consulting and other services accounting for 27 percent. By 1999, accounting and auditing had slipped to 33 percent of total fees, tax was 18 percent and consulting and other services had grown to the an average of 49 percent of the firms' fees.

It is probably harder for education to change than it is for any of the other groups. As one interviewee said, "Business has to be more nimble [than education]. It is shaped quickly by market forces. Higher education is not so nimble—it's only slowly shaped by market forces." Accounting education is burdened by the hierarchy within universities. Before curricula changes can be made, approval must often be given by departmental and college curriculum committees, university administrators, and even boards of regents. Traditional higher education, as represented by liberal arts and humanities, is slow to change by design. Universities like the fact that the bureaucracy protects and insulates them from the real world. Such protection allows universities to withstand change and not worry about such issues as student placement and competition. If you ask philosophy professors, for example, what is going on in the world and how changes are affecting them, they will tell you it is not important to them. They neither worry about student placement nor relevance. Professional schools such as business and law are, in some ways, trapped by this bureaucracy even though they would like to change and be more relevant. They are being pulled in two different directions— toward changes and relevance by the business world and toward insulation and apathy by other parts of the academy.

In recent years, many types of professional schools, including medical schools, law schools, and business schools, have struggled with these competing tensions. Given the battles we have had to fight for change, educators would argue that we have changed significantly. Friends in the professional world, not understanding how difficult change is in academe, argue that we have not changed fast enough.

How Have These Environmental Changes Impacted Education?

In some ways, the implications of change on education are obvious. Schools that are educating students to perform services that have been replaced by technology are finding that their students have a hard time finding jobs and that their student numbers are decreasing rapidly. Schools that have not adapted to change have found that many students who might have chosen accounting as a major in the past are now opting for more popular and highly paid information systems, finance, logistics/supply chain management, e-commerce, and strategy programs. Accounting professionals, who have adapted themselves, tell us that our changes are neither fast nor substantive enough. We are being told that the traditional model underlying accounting education no longer exists.

Historically, our educational model looked something like this:

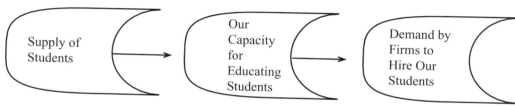

This was a nice model because the supply of students filled our educational pipelines and most of them joined the profession. The traditional hiring model was to serve a short "apprenticeship" in public accounting and then decide whether public accounting, industry, internal audit, or some other work was more attractive, challenging, and rewarding. With supply, capacity, and demand in equilibrium, we neither had to worry about attracting new students—they were always there—nor did we have to worry about placing them. Not only did a few recruiters hire all of our students, but also they each worked hard to get the competitive edge on our campuses through investments of time and resources.

Because of the changes described in this chapter, the model where supply, capacity, and demand are equal no longer exists. In fact, a new, splintered model has emerged that looks like this:

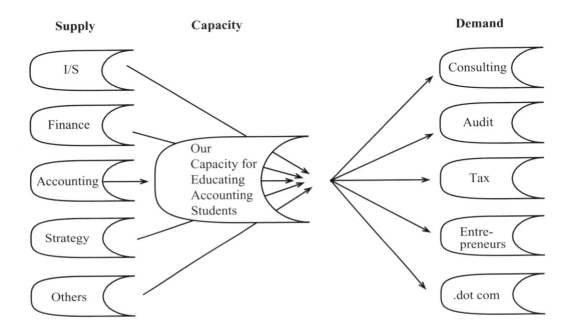

This model makes clear the problems that many of our accounting departments face—we have capacity that was built for a supply/demand market that has changed dramatically. We still have customers for our product, but we have a significantly smaller supply. As a result, other disciplines, such as I/S, Finance, and Strategy, are educating students who are assuming many of the positions previously filled by accounting students. The reduced supply of accounting students is in turn due to the attractiveness of other options for individuals who would have been our students—options that are now readily available to them because of changes that have swept the business world. Ironically, some of the most attractive of these "alternative options" are with the same employers who used to comprise the nucleus of our former market.

The following quotes from one of our interviewees articulate why students in majors other than accounting are being hired to fill accounting positions:

> *It's not the way we would like it to be, but I will tell you the way it is. We will hire any student who has brains, regardless of academic preparation. It's easier to hire smart people, without regard to their academic background, and teach them the accounting they need to know, than it is to search through the smaller pool of accounting-trained people, looking for the same level of native talent. Forty percent of what is traditionally done in an audit doesn't have to be done by partner-track people. The audit function has two fundamental needs: well-educated, bright people who have skills in either (1) business processes or (2) wealth accumulation. The first is handled best by engineering-type people, while the second is handled best by finance-type people.*

The systems-trained people we see can run circles around the accounting-trained people. The top 20 percent of accounting folk are okay, but on the whole, the systems people are more interested, more alert, and just smarter. Why that should be is unclear—is it self-selection? Or, is it something in their education?

How Should Accounting Education Change in Response to Environmental Changes?

In a later chapter, we identify strategies that schools and faculty must take to survive in the changing environment. However, before leaving the topic of changes, it is important to recognize three very important facts. First, accounting education has many positive aspects. Many people believe that accounting education provides the best background for business and other related careers. One focus group participant stated:

I believe that accounting is important, not because of the content, but because of the rigor of the curriculum. It's my personal opinion that the people who we hire who don't have an undergradu- ate accounting degree come in somewhat behind. It's not that they are not as smart, but they don't have as much of the base technical skills to just recognize what they need to do with problems. I think the base technical skills are important, but I think the curriculum is important in the sense that it tends to separate the wheat from the tares. I mean, I really do think that—I almost majored in journalism and what convinced me to major in accounting was that I knew that if I had an accounting degree I could always write, but if I had a journalism degree, I couldn't get an accounting job. My ex-husband was an attorney and he didn't have much accounting background. I can't tell you how many times I spent trying to help him draft merger-acquisition agreements. I'm appalled that there can be a corporate attorney who is very bright and in one of the top law firms who just doesn't get the basic accounting principles. So, I think accounting is a great core curriculum and that we need to build on it with communication skills, analytical skills, and problem-solving skills. —Participant, Atlanta Focus Group

Second, public accounting and industry still see tremendous value in an accounting education and are hiring as many graduates as they can. The AICPA data on supply and demand support the continued value of an accounting education. These data show that even though the pool of account- ing graduates was 20 percent smaller in 1998–99, public accounting firms hired just as many graduates as they did in 1995–96. It is just that they are not paying as much for accounting graduates as they are for other graduates and that students are moving away from accounting to these "higher paying and more exciting" careers and degrees.

Third, if accounting education is to keep up with changes occurring in the business world, educators must understand what types of services their graduates will perform in the future. In our surveys, we asked educators and practitioners what kinds of services would be needed of accounting graduates in the future. When we asked what kind of work they expect accounting graduates to be performing five years from now, *practitioners and educators did not agree*, as shown below.

Ranking of Future Services	Faculty	Practitioners
1. (Most demanded)	Audit	Financial analysis
2.	e-commerce consulting	Financial planning
3.	Systems consulting	Financial reporting
4.	Tax consulting	Strategic consulting
5.	Strategic consulting	Systems consulting

You can see from these responses that faculty still believe audit will be one of the most important services in the future, while practitioners did not rank it in the top five. Both groups identified consulting, analysis, and advising types of services as being most demanded. When we asked what current services will be least demanded in the future, faculty and practitioners agreed that treasury, accounting services, general accounting, and valuation will not be demanded.

When we asked respondents whether they expected the demand for accounting graduates who work in the following types of jobs to decrease, stay about the same, or increase in the future, we received the following responses:

Activity	Faculty: Decrease	Faculty: Stay the Same	Faculty: Increase	Practitioners: Decrease	Practitioners: Stay the Same	Practitioners: Increase
Internal Audit	11.1	**50.8**	38.1	16.4	**60.5**	23.1
Corporate Accounting/ Finance	14.8	**57.5**	27.7	8.8	**55.4**	35.8
Tax	14.0	**61.0**	25.0	9.6	**62.6**	27.8
Audit and Assurance	30.7	**51.2**	18.1	10.6	**70.3**	19.1
Business Consulting and Advising	1.1	10.0	**88.9**	0.4	14.2	**85.4**
Planning and Strategy	1.5	26.4	**72.1**	1.6	25.7	**72.7**

It is clear from the responses to these questions that, while traditional internal audit, corporate accounting/finance, tax, and audit services may not decrease in the future, the real growth opportunities for our graduates are in planning and strategy and business consulting and advising.[6]

Certainly we want to offer students the programs that they need and want and that will add high value in their future. One educator, looking at the salaries being paid by accounting firms and the myriad of new opportunities available to students said:

> As you know, our school has been in the business of educating accountants for some time—that's an understatement, because we have been in the business since the 1900s. I think it is also well known that there are more partners in the larger firms who have degrees from our school than from anywhere else in the world. So, we have been in the business. And to be brutally frank, we would like to stay in this business. But, it is an industry that is in such transition. Our end is in transition—what should we be doing? What should we be doing in the classroom? It's in a state of flux. We are methodically thinking about this issue....We are really grappling with these issues. We think we are doing the right thing now, but we think that what we will be doing in the future is something quite different....From our end, we try to offer students programs that they need and want. And it is increasingly not looking like a no-brainer that we stay in this business. Of course, we all have a lot of respect and...concern for the profession. But that was then and this is now. We feel the pressure, too. We are asking, maybe that's not a business we should be in at all. — Participant, Ross Institute Roundtable

As an educator, think of yourself as someone who is driving 15 miles an hour up a hill in an old pickup truck, pulling a huge load of potatoes on a trailer behind you. You cannot go very fast because your truck is old and the potatoes are heavy. Suddenly, around you zips a new sports car going at least 70 miles per hour. You are envious because you would like to be able to keep up. Yet,

---

6   At first glance, it may appear that faculty responses to this and the prior table are inconsistent. In the results presented in this table, the majority of faculty expects the demand for accounting graduates who work in audit and assurance services to stay the same. In the previous table, faculty believe that accounting graduates will be performing a significant amount of audit-type work five years from now. An explanation for the perceived differences may be that faculty believes that, while the demand for audit and assurance services will not increase, it will not decrease. In addition, faculty probably believe that audit and assurance services play a bigger role in practice today than they really do.

you are tired from working so hard to get the potatoes loaded on the trailer. You say to yourself, "If only I had a car as fast and nimble, I'd be better." In many ways, this scenario is analogous to the situation we face as accounting educators. Everyone in the business world appears to be moving faster than accounting education. Everyone appears to have more money to support change. Other entities appear not to be burdened with the heavy traditions and infrastructures of an institution that does not want to change. Our critics say these are only excuses—that we could make needed changes if we really wanted to. Yet, we look at the old truck and wonder if it will even make the hill. Somehow, we must re-energize ourselves and our educational programs. We have to find a way to shed the heavy load and figure out how to get to the top of the hill faster. To assume that the old truck will not go any faster or that the load must always be pulled may be obsolete assumptions. Fixing the problem first requires that we identify exactly what is causing us to go so slow. In the next three chapters, we look at the three major problems facing accounting education: (1) decreasing students, (2) dissatisfaction of past graduates, and (3) criticisms of our educational model. Once we understand the nature of our problems, we might be able to determine how to make the truck go faster and to fix our problems. In Chapter 6, we identify strategies accounting educators can take to fix the problem and keep up with changes taking place.

CHAPTER 3

Fewer and Less Qualified Students
Are Choosing Accounting as a Major

As stated in Chapter 1, during the past ten years, and continuing through today, we have been bombarded with signals warning us that the future of accounting education is in peril. Some warning signals have been raised by practitioners. Other warning signals have been raised by organizations such as the IMA, AICPA, AECC, and even educators. Because they were only opinions telling us what we did not want to hear, and because the economy has been so strong, it has been easy to discount those warnings. Now, however, more than ever before we have solid evidence of the need for change, evidence that substantiates many of the observations and criticisms we have heard before. Most of this empirical evidence focuses on the number and quality of students choosing to major in accounting.

Data on Enrollments and Graduates

The AICPA has, for many years, conducted a supply-and-demand study, polling schools and employers as to the numbers of students in accounting departments and the numbers of offers made by potential employers.[1] The current year "supply" numbers from the schools are just now in, and they certainly paint a frightening picture. The chart on the next page shows the trend in numbers of students graduating with accounting degrees over the last ten years.

For more than 20 years the number of students obtaining bachelor's and master's degrees in accounting has averaged around 60,000 per year. Unfortunately we do not have comparable data for 1997 and 1998, but we do have the information for the 1999 school year. The number of accounting degrees awarded in the 1998–99 school year fell to 47,600, a decline of 20 percent below the comparable numbers for the 1995–96 school year.[2]

We cannot assume that this one-year graduation record is a fluke and that the numbers will recover tomorrow. The AICPA study also reports that the number of students enrolled in accounting programs is down, from 192,000 in 1995–96 to 148,000 in 1998–99, a 23 percent decline. Most of that decline is in undergraduate students: the number of students pursing Master's in Accountancy

---

[1] *The Supply of Accounting Graduates and the Demand for Public Accounting Recruits—1997* (and the supply portion of the 1999 study), AICPA 1997, 1999.

[2] Prospective employers have recognized this decreasing pool of students and are taking steps to help recruit more accounting students. As a recent article in the *New York Times* stated, "Competing for the smallest pool of college graduates of accounting programs in more than a decade, many of the nation's largest accounting firms and associations have begun grooming talent at secondary schools, the latest battlefield in an industry-wide recruitment war. With scholarships and internships in hand, they are hoping to resuscitate a field that is rapidly losing conscripts to the wonders of technology and the glamour of being an entrepreneur. 'We're making big investments in the development of a high school pipeline,' said a partner at a Big 5 professional services firm who sends recruiters to roughly 3,000 schools a year to scout promising students. 'High school may almost be too late, and at some point we have to start looking at middle schools.'"

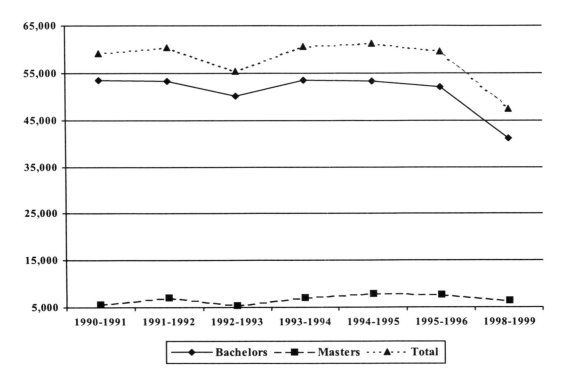

degrees has stayed about the same, perhaps as a result of the 150-hour rule. The number of students pursuing Master's in Taxation degrees fell from 4,000 to 2,000 during the same period. Data from the AICPA Topline Report and a 1990 Gallup Poll show that the percentage of college students majoring in accounting has dropped from 4 percent in 1990 to 2 percent in 2000. Even more alarming, the percentage of high school students who intend to major in accounting has decreased from 2 percent in 1990 to 1 percent in 2000.[3]

Faculty and practitioners who responded to our survey confirmed the data from the AICPA study. We asked three questions relating to quality and quantity of students. The first was asked of both faculty and practitioners and the other two were asked only of faculty. When we asked practitioners and faculty, "Do you believe that there are fewer qualified students majoring in accounting today than five years ago, about the same as five years ago, or more than five years ago?" we received these results:

Number of Students	Faculty Response	Practitioner Response
Fewer qualified students than five years ago	80.1%	45.7%
The same number of qualified students as five years ago	16.6%	42.5%
More qualified students than five years ago	3.3%	11.8%

---

[3] The AICPA retained the Taylor Group to study high school and college students' perceptions about accounting and to help identify why accounting enrollments have decreased. The Group's final report has not been issued. We have been privileged to use their results in this study. In conducting its study, the Taylor Group conducted telephone interviews with over 2,000 high school and college students and held nine focus group sessions around the United States. Their report is referred to as the AICPA Topline Report.

The data referenced in this footnote come from a presentation by Scott Taylor, Chairman of the Taylor Group, to the AICPA Board on July 13, 2000.

The responses to this question, especially from the faculty, support the empirical data assembled by the AICPA. Neither of these pieces of evidence addresses the question of quality, however. That is, they do not really distinguish whether it is quantity only or both quantity and quality of students that are decreasing.

To help us distinguish perceptions about quantity and quality, we asked two additional questions in our faculty survey. When asked whether they thought the *size of the student population* described at their school has decreased, stayed about the same, or increased in the last five years, faculty responded as follows:

Kinds of Students Enrolled	Percent of Faculty Who Responded That the Size of This Student Population Has Decreased	Percent of Faculty Who Responded That the Size of This Student Population Has Stayed the Same	Percent of Faculty Who Responded That the Size of This Student Population Has Increased
Number of students enrolled as *accounting majors*	**63.5**	25.0	11.5
Number of *nonbusiness majors* enrolled in accounting courses	17.9	**52.9**	29.2
Number of students enrolled as *accounting minors*	23.9	**55.5**	20.6
Number of students enrolled as *nonaccounting business majors*	16.9	37.2	**45.9**

When you realize that nearly 300 schools are represented in these responses, these results are frightening. They show that most faculty perceive that the number of accounting majors has decreased, that the number of nonmajors taking accounting classes and enrolling as accounting minors has stayed about the same and that the number of nonaccounting business majors taking accounting classes has increased.

It is apparent from these results that the makeup of students enrolling in accounting classes is different than it was previously. We are teaching proportionately fewer accounting majors and proportionately more nonmajors. This shift in the makeup of our students requires a shift in the way we teach accounting and in the way we manage our departments.

When we asked faculty whether they thought the *quality of the student populations* at their school has decreased, stayed the same, or increased in the last five years, we received the following responses:

Kinds of Students Enrolled	Percent of Faculty Who Responded That the Quality of This Student Population Has Decreased	Percent of Faculty Who Responded That the Quality of This Student Population Has Stayed the Same	Percent of Faculty Who Responded That the Quality of This Student Population Has Increased
Students enrolled as *accounting majors*	**43.7**	38.2	18.1
Students enrolled as *accounting minors*	31.7	**60.7**	7.6
Students enrolled as *nonaccounting business majors*	37.5	**47.3**	15.2

These data suggest that not only is the quantity of our input down, but also that the perceived quality of the smaller group of students choosing accounting as a major is down. Interestingly, it is only the quality of accounting majors that the faculty respondents feel has decreased—the majority of respondents believe that the quality of accounting minors and nonaccounting, business majors has stayed the same. That perception of the decline in quality was supported by the comments of the participants in the Ross Institute Supply and Demand Roundtable. One of those participants, a large-firm recruiter described this decrease in quality when he stated:

By January this year, we had only reached 75 percent of our (hiring) goal. For the first time, we are back on campus interviewing—and that is because of the quality and quantity (of students). To stay with our standards, we are digging deeper.

An experienced faculty member who was a participant in the Ross Institute Roundtable said:

What has clearly happened in our school is that the best student has turned to finance. "Best" is sort of what you remember about the students you were exposed to in the years past.

There was some evidence, provided by department chairs, that contradicted the widespread perceptions of faculty and practitioners about quality of students. The department chairs who responded stated that they believed quality of students, as measured by GPA, SAT/ACT scores, and honors received, has increased during the past ten years. Here are their perceptions:

Measure of Quality	Percent of Department Chairs Who Believe the Quality Measure Was Higher	Percent of Department ChairsWwho Believe the Quality Measure Was Lower	Percent of Department Chairs Who Believe the Quality Measure Was the Same	Percent of Department Chairs Who Stated They Did Not Know Whether the Quality Measure Was Higher or Lower
High school GPA of accounting students in 2000 compared to students enrolled in 1990	32.8	8.6	21.9	36.7
High school GPA of accounting students today compared to those of other business majors today	38.7	1.6	17.7	42.0
SAT/ACT test scores of accounting students today compared to students enrolled in 1990	34.1	9.8	19.5	36.6
Percentage of accounting students receiving honors/ awards today compared to students enrolled in 1990	28.8	12.8	40.0	18.4
SAT/ACT test scores of accounting students today compared to those of other business majors today	32.3	1.6	22.6	43.5

While the largest percent of department chairs responded that they did not know the answers to our quality questions, many responded that quality (measured by test scores, GPAs, and honors/ awards) of students today compared to students enrolled ten years ago—and compared to other business majors—has increased. Obviously, these results are inconsistent with the responses from the faculty and practitioners who responded to our surveys.[4] Their responses are also inconsistent with the comments we heard from focus group respondents and in personal interviews. Setting this conflict aside, we know that—in the best case—the number of students majoring in accounting is down. In the worst case, both the quantity and quality of students electing to major in accounting have decreased.

These are very disturbing data. The dramatic decrease in the number of students choosing accounting as a major and the repeated cries about the quality of entering students being down raise two important strategic questions: (1) why are the decreases occurring, and (2) what do these decreases mean for the future of accounting education?

Why Has the Number of Students Choosing to Major in Accounting Decreased?

There are a number of perceived reasons why the quantity and quality of students choosing to major in accounting have decreased, including: (1) starting salaries for accounting majors are less than for other business majors, (2) students today have more attractive career alternatives than in the past, (3) students today are more willing to choose risky majors than they were in the past, (4) there is a lack of information and considerable misinformation about what accounting is and what accountants do, and (5) the 150-hour rule has increased the opportunity costs to become a CPA and prospective students perceive 150-hour programs as being too narrow and non-value-added.

Decreased Salary Levels

For most of the past ten years, salaries offered by public accounting firms to business school undergraduates have been higher than salaries offered by other finance-related employers; those salary offers were only marginally less than salaries offered by computer and consulting companies. That is no longer true. About four years ago, the salaries offered by both computer-related employers and by consulting firms started to increase rapidly. The chart on the following page, using data published by the National Association of Colleges and Employers (NACE),[5] demonstrates the degree to which salary offers by both public and private accounting employers have decreased relative to the consulting and computer-related companies.

---

[4] Part of the reason for the inconsistency may be that department chairs don't track student quality. When we asked department chairs to provide actual GPA, ACT/SAT, and honors/award data for accounting graduates in 2000 and 1990 and similar data for nonaccounting business majors, very few department chairs responded. Eighteen provided high school GPAs of accounting students in 2000, but only 10 of those respondents had comparable data for 1990. Four provided current high school GPAs of finance, marketing, and management majors, two had current high school GPAs of information systems students, and no one had comparable data for 1990. Thirty-two respondents provided SAT/ACT test scores of accounting students in 2000, but only 24 had comparable data for 1990. Seventeen provided ACT/SAT test scores of finance and marketing students in 2000; 18 provided ACT/SAT test scores of management majors; ten provided ACT/SAT test scores of information systems majors in 2000; but no one had comparable data for 1990. No department chairs provided the number of students receiving honors/awards in either 1990 or 2000. The limited data we received in response to this request was not enough to help us resolve this apparent inconsistency regarding the quality of our students. This lack of knowledge by department chairs about the quality of students in programs is a serious problem. It is difficult to take corrective action unless the nature of student quantity and quality problems is known by those who can best take steps to fix the problem—department chairs. Another explanation is provided by the Taylor Group in their AICPA Topline Report. When they studied the kind of students the profession is attracting, they found that accounting majors were (1) less likely to have taken both AP and college prep courses than college students generally, (2) more likely to have attended community college and currently attend public universities, (3) are more likely to value job security and prestige rather than creativity and working with people, and (4) do report higher GPAs than college students generally. It may be that accounting students actually have higher GPAs but these GPAs were earned by not taking AP and college prep courses and by studying at community colleges.

[5] The data for this chart were developed from the NACE *Salary Survey*, September 30 Reports, recruiting years ended 1990–1999.

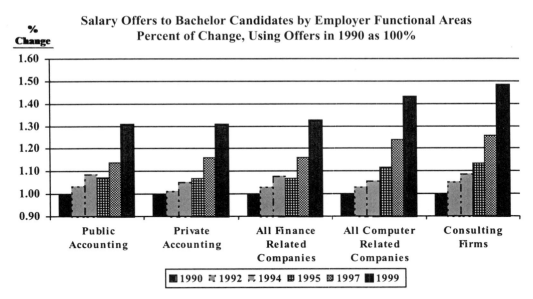

Salary Offers to Bachelor Candidates by Employer Functional Areas
Percent of Change, Using Offers in 1990 as 100%

These data are supported by our survey responses. When we asked department chairs to rank order from highest (1) to lowest (8) and to specify (if they had the information) the average starting salaries of graduates in different undergraduate business programs at their schools, we received the following responses:

Major	Mean Rank	Mean Salary
Information Systems	1.25	$41,402
Accounting	2.42	$35,090
Finance	2.67	$35,400[6]
e-Business	3.17	NA
Logistics/Supply Chain Management	4.30	$30,000
Marketing	4.50	$29,388
Operations	4.76	$38,500 (small sample)

When we asked about starting salaries for graduate programs, we received the following data from department chairs:

Program	Rank	Salary
Master's of Information Systems	1.24	$60,000
Master's of Business Administration	1.85	$48,200
Master's of Accountancy	2.12	$41,200
Master's of Taxation	2.39	$43,800
Master's of Organizational Behavior	4.00	NA
Master's of Public Administration	4.17	NA

These responses suggesting the higher salaries attributable to the M.I.S. and M.B.A. degrees are confirmed by data from the NACE Salary Surveys. The following chart tracks the salary offers made to graduate students, by all employers, from 1990 to 1999.[7]

---

[6] The reason that the rankings of actual salaries and perceived salaries are different is that we received more responses to perceived salaries than we did of actual salaries.

[7] NACE gathers salary offers to M.B.A. candidates, differentiating between those who have one year of experience or less and those who have more than one year of experience between their undergraduate degree and their M.B.A. work. We cite here only the offers made to M.B.A. candidates with one year or less experience.

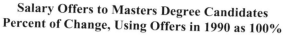

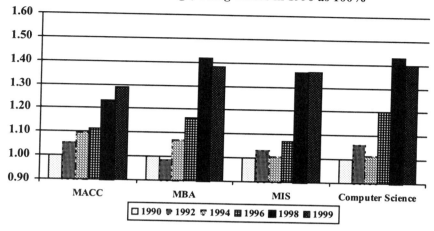

Salary Offers to Masters Degree Candidates
Percent of Change, Using Offers in 1990 as 100%

Legend: □ 1990 1992 1994 1996 ■ 1998 1999

In our surveys, we asked respondents two questions relating to reasons why fewer qualified students were majoring in accounting. When asked "What do you believe are the two main reasons there are fewer students today than five years ago," respondents answered as follows:[8]

Reason Why the Number of Qualified Students Is Down	Most Important Reason— Faculty Responses	Second Most Important Reason— Faculty Responses	Most Important Reason— Practitioner Responses	Second Most Important Reason— Practitioner Responses
Starting salaries are lower than in other disciplines, such as information systems	39.3	15.7	32.3	25.4
Accounting is perceived as less challenging and rewarding than other fields of study	10.9	21.1	23.2	13.4
Students do not understand how challenging and rewarding the accounting profession is	18.3	13.0	6.3	13.4
Accounting is not perceived as having the growth opportunities that other disciplines have	9.6	14.3	11.0	17.4
Accounting is perceived as being backward-looking, while information systems and finance are perceived as being forward-looking	6.6	6.7	9.8	11.2
Accountants are not as respected as other business professionals	1.3	1.8	3.5	9.8
University professors do not do a good job of getting students excited about accounting	2.2	14.6	1.2	4.5

---

[8] The columns in this and the following table do not add to 100 percent because there was an "other" category.

When we asked respondents what were the two most important steps corporations and account-ing firms could take to attract more high-quality students into the accounting profession, the re-sponses were similar:

Action to Attract More Qualified Students	Most Important Action— Faculty Response	Second Most Important Action— Faculty Response	Most Important Action— Practitioner Response	Second Most Important Action— Practitioner Response
Pay higher starting salaries	49.2	14.5	46.8	21.1
Better promote their array of services to students	17.9	22.4	18.9	28.2
Have an increased presence on campus	13.0	16.7	7.3	12.5
Work with high school students	6.9	12.7	8.0	12.7
Work closer with key professors	4.1	13.6	3.6	10.2
Build supplier alliances with key schools	3.3	7.0	3.6	6.0
Change the name of the profession	0.4	2.6	0.5	3.5
Do more advertising	0.0	1.8	3.9	5.0

These responses tell us that the differentials in starting salaries do impact students who are deciding between majors. In fact, we believe the striking increase in salary offers by consulting and computer-related companies is likely to have a greater impact on accounting than on the rest of the business school because accounting programs compete for the same analytically oriented students who are likely to choose information systems or consulting as their majors.

These salary data were confirmed by discussions in our focus groups. Several Big 5 recruiting participants in the focus groups confirmed that salaries within the same firm are higher in the consulting and other emerging tracks than in tax and assurance services. The following quote is typical of these comments.

We used to pay the highest. I remember when I graduated in 1980, I got paid a lot more than my finance friends or other graduates. Now we don't. We have a monopoly on the attest function. Only CPAs can do attest. But, our monopoly service we discount the most. I mean, we're selling jobs at 50 percent. I'll go in for a bid for a client at $100,000 and somebody will come in and underbid me by $50,000. And, then I can't pay the salaries. So the firm says, "We'll pay more when the realization is higher." Their realization is higher in consulting. I had a discussion with a part-ner—a major player at one of the firms—and he believes that when the pain hurts enough, we'll start paying more. —Participant, Los Angeles Focus Group

A department chair at a major school offered a more pessimistic view. He stated that:

Demand for accounting majors from CPA firms looking for auditors is up but supply of students who want to become CPAs is way down. This makes no sense economically. The price being offered to accounting students is too low to satisfy demand. This is true even for four-year bachelor's graduates in accounting compared to other bachelor's graduates. The attestation side of CPA firms can't even compete with their own consulting practices. Add to this the fact that we are phasing in a five-year requirement for CPAs and you have to predict that things will get worse, not better. Who would get a graduate degree in accounting to become CPA qualified when you can make as much or more in most career paths in business schools with a four-year bachelor's degree? If you are paying below the market for top students, why should you expect to hire the top students? Even our master's students are being bid away by other non-CPA employers at much higher prices. —Respondent to our survey

It seems anomalous that the professional firms and industry are clamoring for more and better people, but at the same time their salary offers for accounting students lag the competition. Why should the firms not respond to the decreasing number of accounting graduates by increasing their salary offers? There may be several answers:

- If the firms were to increase starting salaries to competitive levels, they would face a serious compression problem. One major firm recruiter made that point, in a focus group discussion, saying, "It's not a $1 million problem for us, it's a $20 million problem."
- The firms have found that they can hire experienced people, and that their experience justifies a higher billing rate, in turn justifying a higher salary.
- The firms have been able to hire students from other disciplines at lower salaries, and train them in accounting during the summer and on the job.

Whatever the reason, lower salary offers are a problem for accounting education and our ability to attract good students to our schools. We may not be able to convince the professional service firms to raise their salary offers to our traditional students, but we can begin to educate students and guide them toward more attractive career opportunities. We must not wait for the firms to solve our problems. As a partner in one of the Big 5 firms said:

> *So one of the options would be—and it almost sounds like heresy for me to say this—for the accounting groups in schools that can produce the proper talent and drive toward integration to take the lead. They would have to recognize that the principal customer for their students will be elsewhere. If the Big 5 doesn't seem to be able to pay the freight, then [the schools] will have to change their focus to customers who do pay the freight. I hate to say it but if we don't have a message of compensation and work challenge that is worthy of the talent that we keep saying we need, then shame on us.*

More Attractive Career Alternatives than Ever Before

Students entering business schools today have more attractive career alternatives than did students in the past. The result is increased competition for accounting programs and more difficulty attracting bright students. Students entering business schools today can choose from new, attractive majors that did not exist previously. Some of these new majors are information systems, e-business, logistics/supply chain management, strategy, and various types of finance specialties. These majors not only prepare students for new and exciting careers that have developed because of globalization, increased competition and technology, they also prepare students for work now performed by firms that have historically recruited primarily accounting students—the professional service firms and "finance" departments in corporations. The following quote from a focus group participant illustrates the degree to which students are choosing these new majors:

> *I was at a career fair yesterday and the line for every booth to talk to the consulting people was 50 people long. Every so often we would get one lone accounting major who would come over and talk to us who represented assurance and tax.* —Participant, Atlanta Focus Group

Students Are More Willing to Choose Risky Majors and Career Tracks than Before

Decreases in enrollments are partly due to the extraordinarily strong economy we have experienced in the past few years. Choosing accounting as a major used to be seen as a safe educational choice because it provided a predictable entrée into the larger business world, either through an extended internship with a CPA firm or into the general management program of one of the larger corporations. Given the strength of the economy, however, students are now less concerned about safety and predictability in their career planning and more interested in challenge and the potential for growth and wealth accumulation. The strength of the economy has changed students' expectations dramatically, to the extent that they are not worried about the prospects of changing companies or even careers. The idea of stability is now stultifying rather than reassuring. Students now expect that they will get richer and be more successful than ever before. Today, students are willing to assume greater career risks, believing that if their first career choice fails, other alternatives will await them. This perception about students was well articulated by one of our focus group members who said:

> *One thing we notice in recruiting is that today's students have never seen a bad job market. They've never seen downsizing and layoffs. In 1990, when I graduated, we were lucky to find a job. Students today believe they have the world at their fingertips, with an unending stream of opportunities.* —Participant, New York Focus Group

Not only are students more tolerant of risk, but the actual risk of making a wrong career choice in today's circumstances is also low. In addition, the potential pay-off from a risky choice is seen as very high. One focus group participant who was a recruiter stated that she had been pursuing an accounting graduate, but was losing her. The student asked "if this dot.com opportunity doesn't work out, can I come back to you in a couple of years?" The recruiter was forced to admit that the answer was "of course."

Misinformation and Lack of Information about Accounting and Accounting Careers

For years, accountants have been thought of cynically as individuals who "wear green eye shades, are narrow and boring, who work alone and who do tedious numbers-related work." Accounting educators and accounting practitioners know that image is incorrect. However, do prospective students know this? According to the AICPA Topline Report, apparently not. After studying both high school and college students, the research firm stated the following:

> *Most students, even those pursuing an accounting degree, are ignorant of the basics of an accounting career. They cannot accurately describe the work of an accountant, their responsibilities, their opportunities or the types of firms an accountant might work for. Students can differentiate, to some extent, between a general accountant and a CPA, but their perceptions are based on credentials alone—that credential must afford a CPA some measure of prestige. "CPAs are higher than general accountants because they are certified." These same students were not ignorant of other careers.*

> *While students do, generally, have specific career interests, much of their information regarding careers, especially accounting, is somewhat faulty as exemplified by this statement from a high school student: "A CPA is someone who works for the government."*

> *A CPA license, as opposed to advanced degrees, such as an M.B.A., is seen by many students as limiting their career options, rather than expanding them. "It seems like you can do a lot more if you get an M.B.A....If you get a CPA, you have to be an accountant, but if you get an M.B.A., you can do anything you want." "I can't see any applications for accounting, except being an accountant."*

> *Students are becoming turned off early. Our research shows that students are making these decisions (about careers and majors) earlier and earlier. Most students are deciding on a college major during their college-application process. Many do not consider accounting because they've never been exposed to it (no classes, except bookkeeping available in high school), and others rule out accounting because they perceive it to be a profession (bookkeeping) for people who do not continue on to college. And even some students who find value in accounting—and have chosen accounting as their major—do not find value in continuing on for their CPA.*

> *For students, accounting is most often associated with money, numbers, math, and taxes. And except for the rare math-and-details-oriented student, these are not positive attributes. Accountants are seen as doing boring, tedious, and monotonous number-crunching, by themselves, in a cubicle. As one accounting major stated, "If you are a detailed-oriented person who likes to work by yourself, then it's for you." While accounting and business majors are, not surprisingly, somewhat more positive regarding accounting, even they see accounting as a necessary evil. "It's a dirty job, but somebody has to do it." In fact, many choose accounting because of the negative*

perceptions, thinking that these negative perceptions must lead to higher demand for accountants, greater job security, and possible higher pay. "Accounting is something that is in demand, because no one wants to do it."

As is evident from these quotes, high school and college students do not perceive accounting and accounting careers as being very positive.[9] These misperceptions may be causing us to attract the wrong kind of students into accounting. As one focus group member said:

One of the things we need to do is attract a different type of person into accounting. I think that starts out in high school. I remember a colleague who got in the profession because he said, "I got in because I always wanted the correct answer." When they go into accounting, they always want to feel like "don't tell me how to do it, just give me the answer." Well, in practice, there is no right answer. —Participant, Los Angeles Focus Group

This lack of correct information about accountants and accounting is serious because students' perceptions of accounting are not compatible with the creative, rewarding, people-oriented careers that many students envision for themselves.[10] Accounting is seen—even by those who choose accounting as their major and their potential career—as hard work and a good career for math lovers. If, because of these perceptions, we attract the wrong kinds of students, those students will not meet the needs of accounting and other firms, thus further hurting the reputation of accounting majors. Furthermore, they will not be happy with the direction the profession is going.

This lack of information is probably caused by four factors: (1) misunderstanding of what accounting careers are like by high school guidance counselors and others, (2) bad definitions of what accounting is and the kinds of skills it takes to be successful as an accountant on career choice and aptitude tests administered to high school students, (3) high school "accounting" courses that give students the impression that accounting and bookkeeping are the same and that perpetuate the perception that accountants are scorekeepers,[11] and (4) introductory accounting courses that give college students the impression that accounting is a narrow field and that accountants are only scorekeepers.

While accounting educators may not be able to make an immediate difference with all of these problems, we can and must impact introductory accounting classes. Consider the following comment from the AICPA Topline Report:

---

[9] Hardin et al. (2000) surveyed 128 influential high school teachers from 40 states regarding their views of accounting, engineering, law, and medicine on 24 attributes. They found that high school educators have a relatively low opinion of accounting as a career option for high school students. According to the authors (Hardin, O'Bryan, and Quirin), "although there were a few positive results (e.g., level of ethics), the overall picture that emerges is an unfavorable one for the accounting profession." O'Bryan spent part of his sabbatical last fall visiting high schools to educate students about opportunities in the accounting profession. He found three major hurdles in changing high school teachers' and students' perceptions of the accounting profession. First, it is difficult to get the message that accounting is a challenging and rewarding career to the teachers who interact with the best and brightest students. Second, when accounting is offered in high schools, it is offered as part of a vocational track. Third, many students told him that their counselors had discouraged them from taking high school accounting because it was not for college-bound students.

[10] When the Taylor group asked students what were the most important things they considered in choosing a career, they found that both high school and college students identified the four top elements of an attractive career as one that is (1) personally rewarding, (2) involves working with people, (3) had a good home/work balance, and (4) involved them making a contribution to society. Students' perceptions were that accounting ranked low on all of these characteristics.

[11] According to Scott Taylor of the Taylor Group, only 65 percent of all U.S. high schools offer accounting courses. Of the students who enter college from the 35 percent of high schools that do not offer accounting courses, 17 percent will take a college accounting course. Of the students who attend the 65 percent of high schools that do offer accounting courses, only 25 percent of those students take high school accounting and of those, only 15 percent continue on to take a college accounting class. In those schools that offer accounting, only 9 percent of the 75 percent who do not take high school accounting will take a college accounting class. These results provide evidence that students who attend high schools that offer accounting courses and even students who take accounting in high school are no more likely to take a college accounting class than those who attend high schools that do not teach accounting. It appears that having a high school accounting class does not encourage students to study accounting in college.

*Compounding this problem (misinformation) are poor introductory accounting courses (and pro-
fessors) where you work problem after problem—alone. "I know they are just intro classes, but I
thought I would be able to learn something that I would be able to use." Important is what is not
portrayed in introductory accounting courses. Accounting is not portrayed as a creative profession, nor is it portrayed as a profession where you work with other people, in an advisory role, to
solve problems.*

The first two courses in accounting too often focus on mechanics and fail to give the students a
glimpse of the benefits of a more exciting and comprehensive accounting curriculum.[12] Not only is
a mechanical approach seen as dull, it turns off the more creative students and encourages and
rewards those students who find comfort in mechanics. Our course workload has a reputation as being
demanding. If it is perceived as both demanding and mechanical, it is no wonder that our classes are
less and less attractive to prospective students.

The 150-Hour Rule Has Increased the Opportunity Cost for Students

Given the changes taking place in the profession, the 150-hour rule is almost universally seen as
a mistake. It is seen largely as a rule that both increases opportunity costs and forces students to
specialize at a time when they should not specialize. In today's market, the opportunity cost to
become an accountant—or at least to qualify for a CPA license—is too high. Many professionals we
talked to either said (1) it was the right idea, but has been implemented badly (accounting educators
have just added more of the same),[13] or (2) the idea was right at the time, but that the underlying
vision—the notion of education for an accounting profession—is no longer compelling.[14] Regardless of how we were motivated to add a fifth-year requirement, almost everyone agrees that most
150-hour programs are not appropriate now, especially where we have added a fifth year of more
detailed accounting to an already too technical course of study. While focus group participants
strongly communicated this feeling, the lack of value of a fifth year has also been clearly communicated by the market—as demonstrated by the NACE salary data for Master's of Accountancy
candidates, cited earlier in this chapter. Given the attractiveness of other career options, and the extra
burden of another year in school pursuing the same subjects in more depth, it is, once again, no
wonder that enrollments are down.

---

[12] For a discussion of the type of introductory accounting course that has been recommended by past studies, see Position
Statement Number 2 of the Accounting Education Change Commission.

[13] In fact, as you will see in the next chapter, only 4.3 percent of educators and 14.3 percent of practitioners believe that
having a bachelor's degree only is sufficient to be a professional accountant. 95.7 percent of educators and 85.7 percent
of practitioners would recommend some kind of advanced degree to be an accountant. In addition, the Taylor Group
found that 76 percent of high school students and 80 percent of college students plan to attend some kind of graduate
school (this compares with only 57 percent in 1990.) When asked whether their choice of career would be influenced by
whether they had to spend an additional year in college beyond a bachelor's degree, 78 percent of high school students
and 85 percent of college students stated that they would still choose the same career. Further, when asked specifically
whether the requirements to become a CPA (including the 150-hour requirement) seemed fair, 71 percent of high school
students, 81 percent of college students, and 80 percent of college students who switched from accounting to another
major stated that they thought the requirements were fair. When asked specifically about the 150-hour requirement, only
26 percent of high school, 5 percent of college, and 9 percent of switchers stated that the 150-hour requirement would
even enter into their decision to become a CPA. Looking at these data, it appears that the 150-hour requirement has less to
do with the decrease in the number of students than does beginning salaries or misinformation. As you will see in
Chapter 5, the problem is not with the 150-hour requirement but with the kinds of requirements universities have
implemented to fulfill the 150-hour programs.

[14] An alternative reason why five-year programs have not been widely subscribed to is the explanation of "disruptive
technologies" written about by Clayton Christensen of the Harvard Business School. Using disk drives as an example, he
says that it is not always the best products that carry the day. While some disk drive manufacturers are adding more "bells
and whistles" to computers, making them as powerful as possible, most consumers do not use all the capabilities of the
computer. As a result, other manufacturers become very successful with products that are not nearly as good or powerful,
but which are less expensive. These "disruptive technologies" can eliminate the market for superior products. It may be
that five-year accounting degrees are superior products that may not be necessary, especially given the changes we are
experiencing in the business world. Other majors and disciplines, with shorter graduation requirements and lower barriers
of entry but that are less costly, may be disruptively stealing our market share.

Concluding Comments

It is tempting to look for someone or something to blame for the 20+ percentage drop in accounting majors. However, given the complex nature of the problem, that would be counter-productive. These drops in enrollment pose serious threats to our accounting departments and schools. Some schools have already faced serious declines in resources and faculty. Other schools may not be far behind. Equally important, we could very well face classes that will attract less interesting and challenging students.[15] We can complain about the forces that have brought this threat upon us but, as satisfying as that might be, it will not change the facts. Obviously, there are many reasons why the number of students choosing to major in accounting has decreased. Some of those reasons are due to our inability or unwillingness to prepare students for changing careers. Some of those reasons have to do with the changing nature of the work that accountants perform and by the emergence of technology that has eliminated the need for traditional accounting work. Some have to do with the increasingly closer alignment of other disciplines and curricula with the changing nature of accounting work. As accountants move more from preparation of financial information to analysis and use of financial information, the curricula of other disciplines such as information systems and finance may actually align closer with what accountants do than does accounting curricula. Some are due to the relative decrease in starting salaries and the perceived psychological and financial rewards from practicing as accountants. Some are due to a lack of accurate information about the types of work that accountants do.

What is important is interpreting what is causing the declining enrollments and deciding how to respond. One of our interviewees said, "Each school will have to decide for itself what the decline means for its programs." In Chapter 6, we provide specific ideas about how schools can respond.

We can commiserate and fret about the decline in enrollments, hoping they are temporary or that they will not significantly impact the number of students in our programs or that enrollments will not worsen significantly until we retire. However, the empirical evidence is compelling. Whether we like it or not, the number of students electing to major in accounting has decreased and we are now teaching proportionately more nonaccounting business majors than ever before. In some ways, our role has already switched more from educating majors to performing a service function for other business school majors. As enrollments continue to decline, we can continue the transition to a service role or we can try to determine how to make our accounting curricula and degrees more attractive to prospective students. Hopefully, professionals will find ways to reward graduates so that they are competitive with graduates from other disciplines. While we can't do much about the profession, we can make changes within academia that will be more responsive to our students— changes that will reverse the decline in enrollments and allow accounting to occupy the preeminent position it has traditionally held within business schools.

---

[15] Some accounting faculty who responded believe we are already attracting less interesting and challenging students. As one faculty member stated, "I teach both M.B.A. and M.Acc. students and the contrast is significant. At my school, several of the best accounting faculty are now opting for teaching in the M.B.A. program rather than the M.Acc. because 'that is where the action is.'"

CHAPTER 4

Why Accounting Practitioners and Educators Would Not Major in Accounting Again

Sales experts long ago concluded that "word of mouth" and "personal testimonials" are the best types of advertising. The Taylor Group[1] found this to be true when they asked high school and college students what they intended to study in college. Their study found that students were more likely to major in accounting if they knew someone, such as a friend or relative, who was an accountant. But what would happen if those who are accountants—either accounting educators or practitioners—quit advocating accounting as a career and major and instead recommended that other majors and careers were more attractive? It appears from our research that we are about to find out. Although nearly 100 percent of accounting educators and 79 percent of accounting practitioners who responded to our surveys had undergraduate degrees in accounting, most of them stated that *they would not get an accounting degree if completing their education over again*. When asked "If you could prepare for your professional career by starting college over again today, which of the following would you be most likely to do?" the responses were as follows:

Type of Degree	% of Educators Who Would	% of Practitioners Who Would
Earn a bachelor's degree in something other than accounting and then stop	0.0	7.8
Earn a bachelor's degree in accounting, then stop	4.3	6.4
Earn a Master's of Business Administration (M.B.A.) degree	37.7	36.4
Earn a Master's of Accountancy degree	31.5	5.9
Earn a Master's of Information Systems degree	17.9	21.3
Earn a master's degree in something else	5.4	6.4
Earn a Ph.D.	1.6	4.4
Earn a J.D. (law degree)	1.6	11.4

These results are frightening, especially considering the fact that we are moving quickly toward a universal application of the rule requiring 150 hours to practice as a CPA, and that the most popular educational model used to prepare CPA candidates is a Master's of Accountancy degree. At the same time we are recommending that students get a Master's of Accountancy degree (M.Acc.), only 5.9 percent of practicing accountants would get a M.Acc. if they were starting their education

---

[1] The AICPA Topline Report concluded that "Students who have friends and family who are accountants are much more knowledgeable regarding accounting and, correspondingly, much more likely to consider accounting as a career."

over again. Even more amazing is that the largest proportion of accounting faculty members feels the same way. It is telling that six times as many practicing accountants would get an M.B.A. as would an M.Acc., over three times as many practitioners would get a Master's of Information Systems degree as would get an M.Acc., and nearly twice as many practitioners would get a law degree instead of an M.Acc. Together, only 12.3 percent (6.4% + 5.9%) of practitioners would get either an undergraduate or graduate degree in accounting.[2] This decrease in the perceived value of accounting degrees by practitioners is captured in the following quotes:

> *We asked a financial executive what advice he would give to a student who wanted to emulate his career. We asked him if he would recommend a M.Acc. degree. He said, "No, I think it had better be broad. Students should be studying other courses and not just taking as many accounting courses as possible. If they're going to do that, they should plan to be one of the enforcers. They should plan on working for the SEC and trying to be one of their generals. And, if I was going to counsel someone with regard to career, I would urge them to get some operations experience along the way."* —Interviewee

> *My job right now is no longer putting numbers together. I do more analysis. My finance skills and my M.B.A. come into play a lot more than my CPA skills.* —Participant, CPA Vision Focus Group

> *I have been on the advisory board of XYZ University...and we have been asking ourselves, "What are the needs of today's accountants?" The IT world is meshing very closely with the accounting world, in practice, and so we are creating a new course of study that will combine accounting and information technology into one unique major....In my mind, that's the way to go.* —Interviewee

> *I always felt like accounting people were a part of it [central role in the company]. Now I see us moving away from that. The information systems department was smaller than ours when I started. Now their department is way bigger than ours, and they're the trainers. My mentor wants me to get a CMA, but I want to learn about information systems.* —Participant, CPA Vision Focus Group

The preference for the M.B.A. degree over a Master's of Accountancy degree is motivated both by the nature of the degree and the degree title. When we asked whether "A Master's of Business Administration (M.B.A.) degree title is more valuable than a Master's of Accountancy (M.Acc.) degree title for accounting graduates," 49.0 percent of accounting educators stated that they either somewhat or strongly agreed, while only 32.4 percent of accounting educators responded that they either somewhat or strongly disagreed. In contrast, 64.5 percent of accounting practitioners either somewhat or strongly agreed with the statement that the M.B.A. title is more valuable, while only 15.3 percent of respondents either somewhat or strongly disagreed.

Having accounting practitioners and educators state that they would prefer other degrees to accounting degrees is similar to the owner of a BMW or, worse yet, a BMW salesperson telling her children and friends that if she had the buying decision to do over again, she would purchase a different kind of car next time around. If those who practice and teach accounting cannot provide positive testimonials about the value of accounting degrees, then who can?

The responses to our survey questions reveal that accounting practitioners view accounting education and accounting degrees less positively than do accounting educators. This perceived difference in the value of accounting degrees between practitioners and educators may be part of the problem. As educators, we can argue that practitioners really do not understand all the good things we are doing, but that protest quickly becomes hollow when we understand the monumental input

---

[2] We did not ask respondents how many would get various combinations of degrees such as undergraduate accounting and Master's of Business Administration degrees. Such combinations could increase the demand for undergraduate accounting degrees. In fact, the Taylor Group found that while very few students rank having a CPA as attractive, about half found having both a CPA and M.B.A. to be attractive.

and output problems we are facing. While it may be difficult for us to admit that our programs are off the mark, the decreasing demand for our programs certainly supports the practitioner viewpoint. If we cannot convince ourselves to believe the opinions expressed by critics, we must be convinced by the empirical evidence regarding the decrease in student demand for our educational programs.

Why Accounting Practitioners and Educators Would Not Major in Accounting Again

While the evidence that accounting practitioners and educators view other degrees as more attractive than accounting degrees is frightening, the follow-up question "Why do they feel that way?" is a more useful inquiry. It takes significant pain for accounting graduates to admit that something they worked so hard for has less value than other alternatives today. It is probably more difficult for educators to admit that their own preferences may not have been right. We cannot take proactive steps to fix the problem until we know what is causing these perceptions. While empirical evidence rarely answers the question "Why," we gained valuable insights into their reasons from our personal interviews, background readings, and focus group meetings.

Some of the reasons accounting practitioners and educators would not major in accounting today are very closely related to the reasons why students do not choose accounting as a major (as were discussed in Chapter 3). While all of those reasons apply here as well, there is a big difference between "perceptions of prospective accounting students" and "perceptions of people who already have accounting degrees." We can argue that prospective students suffer from misinformation or a lack of information and really do not understand the excitement provided by accounting education and accounting careers. However, those "misinformation" arguments do not work with practicing accountants and accounting educators. It is those who have the most knowledge about accounting degrees and careers—current accountants who majored in accounting—that we are addressing here. If anyone has an accurate picture of the value of an accounting degree, they do. There appear to be two major reasons why knowledgeable accounting educators and practitioners would not major in accounting again. One reason has to do with the nature of accounting education and one has to do with the nature of accounting work as stated here:

1. The business world has changed dramatically, while accounting education has not. Accounting education is perceived as being too narrow and backward-looking and too costly for the benefits received.

2. The idea of a career in accounting has lost favor because of technological and competitive changes. Business people who want an interesting and rewarding career are looking elsewhere.

The business world has changed dramatically, while accounting education has not. Accounting education is perceived as being too narrow and backward-looking and too costly for the benefits received.

None of us would assert that the business world is the same as it was 15 years ago. The difficulty is in knowing *how* it has changed and *how* we should react to those changes. The following three quotes are typical of what we heard from practicing accountants and educators about the changes taking place.

The world economy is entering a new and highly complex era. Technology is becoming an ever-increasing driver of strategy and decision making. More and more, companies and individuals must compete in a global marketplace. At the same time, businesses and individuals are inundated with data and information from a variety of sources. Success in this environment is increasingly dependent on the strategic management and use of knowledge to understand and analyze this flood of information, and to create and realize value. *Mastering knowledge in today's global marketplace requires an increasing emphasis on the understanding of a broad range of business competencies.*

XYZ Discussion Draft, —AICPA (emphasis added)

Now everybody wants and expects more. What they're looking for is for our people to have better business minds, to be able to think broader, to be more innovative, to share best practices and, if they are not getting that from their service providers, I think they're concerned because in today's business, every small edge counts. And, the stakes are so big for them that they've raised the bar very, very high for us. —Participant, New York Focus Group

We've gone from only performing some narrow roles that people think they understand as being accounting roles to being many other roles that outsiders aren't really clear whether it's the accountant who does it or not. And with it, with the advances in technology and so forth, have come even greater needs for accountants to do more and more, but also greater needs for all of us as stakeholders, to get the message out that today there is a different definition of what an accountant is. —Participant, New York Focus Group

Robert Elliott, KPMG partner and current chairman of the AICPA, speaks often about the value that accountants can and should provide. He identifies five stages of the "value chain" of information. The first stage is recording business events. The second stage is summarizing recorded events into usable data. The third stage is manipulating the data to provide useful information. The fourth stage is converting the information to knowledge that is helpful to decision makers. The fifth and final stage is using the knowledge to make value-added decisions. He uses the following diagram to

illustrate this value chain:

| **Stage 1** | **Stage 2** | **Stage 3** | **Stage 4** | **Stage 5** |

This five-stage breakdown is a helpful analysis of the information process. However, the frightening part of Mr. Elliott's analysis is his judgment as to what the segments of the value chain are worth in today's world. Because of the impact of technology, he believes that:

- Stage 1 activity is now worth no more than $10 per hour
- Stage 2 activity is now worth no more than $30 per hour
- Stage 3 activity is now worth $100 per hour
- Stage 4 activity is now worth $300 per hour
- Stage 5 activity is now worth $1,000 per hour

In discussing this value chain, Mr. Elliott urges the practice community to focus on upper-end services, and he urges us to prepare our students so they aim toward that goal as well. Historically, accounting education has prepared students to perform stage 1- and stage 2-type work. We spend significant amounts of time teaching recording and summarizing functions, and how to prepare financial statements. Think about the typical curricula:

- The first accounting course is usually a prep course in financial accounting for the intermediate, which covers the nature of debits and credits and how to prepare financial statements. The second course in management accounting is usually a prep course for cost accounting.
- The intermediate accounting and cost accounting courses focus students on tracking costs and the preparation of financial reports on the basis of those costs. The orientation is usually rule-based and requires significant amounts of memorization.
- The advanced courses are often focused on more detail in tax, auditing, financial, and cost accounting.

One senior faculty member, commenting on the idea of an information value chain, said this:

Accounting has traditionally been taught moving up the value chain, starting at the recording process. It gives students a bitter taste for accounting and attracts a narrow student. My observation, based on my work in the AAA and on accreditation committees, is that the vast majority of academe hasn't bought into the idea of teaching toward the top of the value chain, and accounting continues to be taught from bottom up. —Participant, Ross Institute Roundtable

If technology has replaced the needs and minimized the rewards of performing stage 1 and stage 2 work, has not technology also eliminated the need to teach students how to perform detailed work at these early stages? Consider the following quotes:

The role of management accountants is very different in 1999. Growing numbers of management accountants spend the bulk of their time as internal consultants or business analysts within their companies. Technological advances have liberated them from the mechanical aspects of accounting. They spend less time preparing standardized reports and more time analyzing and interpreting information. Many have moved from the isolation of accounting departments to be physically positioned in operating departments with which they work. Management accountants work on cross-functional teams, have extensive face-to-face communications with people throughout their organizations, and are actively involved in decision making. —IMA, *Counting More, Counting Less*

It's a different way of thinking today—it's a futuristic thinking, rather than a historical thinking. Twenty years ago, cost accounting was after-the-fact keeping track of what something cost to make and today it's out working with suppliers trying to get a cost down so that your company can buy the product cheaper. The whole perspective has changed. It's futuristic. That's where the accounting information has value—not in the historical. —Participant, Los Angeles Focus Group

Students need to know how to analyze. An accounting student needs to know that there are technical rules and regulations. He or she doesn't need to be able to tell me what FAS 124 is. I don't even know what FAS 124 is, but I if I need to know it, I know where to get it. They need to know that there's a body of rules and regulations that govern the practice of accounting, both within business and within the profession. They need to understand financial statements. They need to understand how to read them and they need to understand what is in them. —Participant, Chicago Focus Group

While the world has changed dramatically, there are strong feelings that accounting education has not kept up. In our survey we asked, "How well is accounting education today meeting the needs and expectations of accounting professionals?" The response, with 4 representing "very well," was 2.69 from both faculty and practice respondents. But others have been more outspokenly critical, as these quotes demonstrate:

Although school and faulty competencies have advanced, the gap between practice and academic research and teaching has widened. The lack of business interaction, changing technologies, aging faculty, and shortage of incentives to change have inhibited faculty initiative for change that is necessary to keep pace with a rapidly changing environment....The pace of change in the external environment is too high for some faculty and many are not investing in lifelong learning for themselves. Often they rely too much on old methods and, lacking direct interaction with industry, generate little cutting-edge research that makes a difference to industry. —AACSB Leadership Report

CEOs have come to see accountants as being 90% concerned with external financial reporting—and the audits thereof. And neither of those activities has anything to do with the way managers run the business. From the standpoint of the CEO, the accounting profession (and accounting education) has been marginalized. Today's successful CFO grew up in a different milieu than the typical accountant. Today's CFO will have been an analyst or a systems person. They understand the elements of the business, but they also understand how management peers make decisions, and the information they need to make those decisions—with forward-looking information. Accountants have lost sight of who their customers are and so have lost their relevance. It is relatively easy to hire people who can be charged with the responsibility for financial reporting. They can do their job and be ignored. —Interviewee

The most critical work activities for management accountants today are strategic planning and process improvement; neither is taught in accounting curricula. Accounting educators must be sure that their students acquire the necessary KSAs to perform these and other key work activities. To better meet the needs of their students and corporate customers, college and university account-ing educators should obtain a better understanding of the work performed in modern corporations. —IMA, *Counting More, Counting Less*

The Vision Project has huge implications for education. A distinction should be made between the traditional education to enter the profession and nontraditional skills. On the traditional side, there are a number of positive curriculum changes at a number of institutions. However, many schools still train people only to prepare and audit financial statements. While this is a core service of the profession, the education is not broad enough to equip graduates to take advantage of all of the opportunities the Vision Project identified. "Steering A Course for the Future," —Interview with Robert Elliott, as he assumed the chairmanship of the AICPA.

A major firm recruiter provided a more positive perspective, but with a serious caveat:

From my perspective there has been a lot of positive change in education. As we look at communi-cation skills and technology skills, and so on, students are far better prepared to be in today's business climate than they were five or ten years ago. So the change has been terrific, quite honestly. I think the message is that we'd like to see those changes be more pervasive and that there's an opportunity to do even more. Actually, it's critical that we do more if our students are going to be competitive, the way that the business world is going. It is essential that we keep the foot on the accelerator with regard to change. —Participant, New York Focus Group

As the work of accountants has changed, other, often shorter and less difficult, majors are preparing students to work as "accountants." With technology now performing the recording and summarizing functions, there is no significant market or competitive advantage to pursuing a rigor-ous, rule-based curricula. One Big 5 recruiter summarized this problem well.

The other [nonaccounting] majors that are coming out of school today are bringing to bear the things that accountants have traditionally done in the past. I think what you're seeing now is a difficulty in differentiating majors coming out of school—a finance major from an accountant, for example. As a result, it continues to be a challenge for us as a firm as to what we are looking for in the qualities of graduates and the approach we take when looking for people to join our organiza-tion. —Participant, New York Focus Group

We can summarize this problem by using the following Venn diagram.

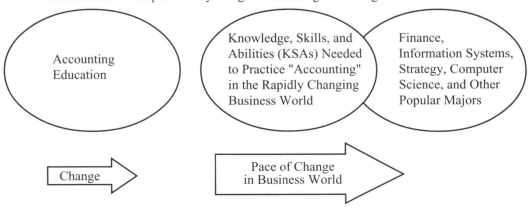

Accounting Major	Relevant Education	M.B.A., Finance, and Information Systems

This diagram illustrates the two changes that are occurring and causing practitioners and educators to choose not to major in accounting today: (1) accounting education is not changing fast enough to keep up with changes in the business world, and (2) as the business world changes, increasingly more of the knowledge, skills and abilities (KSAs) needed to do what "accountants" do are being taught by other, often lower cost, disciplines. Students studying finance and information systems, for example, can get a four-year degree that some would argue is less rigorous than an accounting degree and be well prepared to perform many of the services that are now being performed by professional service firms and corporate accountants.

To understand the attractiveness of related majors, we asked our survey respondents to rank the attractiveness of various business majors and to think about how the accounting major might be changed to make it more attractive. Their responses to those questions bear out their dislike for the accounting major as it has been traditionally taught.

Question Asked	Faculty Who Strongly Disagreed or Disagreed	Faculty Who Agreed or Strongly Agreed	Practitioners Who Strongly Disagreed or Disagreed	Practitioners Who Agreed or Strongly Agreed
Accounting is a more attractive college major than finance	35.7%	38.6%	30.0%	49.5%
Accounting is a more attractive college major than information systems	55.2	22.8	49.7	31.1
Accounting and information systems should be combined into one college major	25.0	57.5	34.7	52.0
Accounting and finance should be combined into one college major	38.7	41.2	28.7	58.6
The various business majors are too isolated from each other	21.3	62.3	29.6	47.3
Accounting education is integrated sufficiently with other business disciplines	53.3	25.0	38.6	36.4

In summary, it appears that both practicing accountants and educators believe: (1) accounting education has not changed enough to meet the changing needs of accountants, (2) that other majors may now be preparing students as well or better for the work accountants now do, and (3) that accounting education is too isolated from other business disciplines. These feelings are strong enough to convince them that they would not get an accounting degree if starting over again today.

The idea of a career in accounting has lost favor because of technological and competitive changes. Business people who want an interesting and rewarding career are looking elsewhere.

A second reason why practicing accountants and educators would not study accounting today is because of problems they perceive with accounting careers. The problems most often mentioned in our research were:

1. Technology has made much of what accountants do obsolete and the demand for the traditional work of accountants, audit and tax, has decreased.

2. Accounting careers are less attractive financially than other careers.

3. There is less psychic income from being an accountant than there used to be and the CPA brand is not worth what it was previously.

Technology Has Made Much of What Accountants Do Obsolete and the Demand for the Traditional Work of Accountants, Audit and Tax, Is Not Increasing

One of the most pervasive themes we heard in our research was that technology has replaced much of what accountants have historically done. No one is impressed by a neat set of financial statements anymore—all of the gathering, recording, and reporting can now be done more efficiently using any of a number of inexpensive software packages. One observer said:

What used to be a skill is no longer an important skill and that is true whether accounting is outsourced or whether it is an internal, shared service. No matter where it's done, it is done by somebody's data-processing system. If it's outsourced, it appears on a screen on your desk. If it's done by a box underneath your desk, it's still available on a screen. Now, the focus has to be on being able to interpret and use the information provided on the screen. —Interviewee

As we suggested in Chapter 2, practitioners who saw this technology revolution coming have repositioned themselves as interpreters and called themselves finance professionals, information consultants, or decision-support specialists. Practitioners who have not made the transition have been relegated to mechanical, uninspiring, and unrewarding jobs. The fear of being left behind in one of those jobs has motivated both the IMA and AICPA to push their members to move up the information value chain.

One focus group participant said:

As you know, the IMA changed its journal and called it Strategic Finance *instead of* Management Accountant. *It is my view that the term finance is a broader umbrella under which accounting resides. I do use the terms interchangeably, but I guess if I had to pick one term, I would say that I work in finance without necessarily thinking about it.* —Participant, Atlanta Focus Group

Another focus group participant said it this way:

Accounting is like baseball. The game has not changed substantially in 100 years. But what has changed is the expectations of team owners, the players, and the fans on the one hand and the incredible number of tools we now have to deliver the game on the other hand. With more tools to deliver the product, you can come up with an incredible array of additional statistics that people can now recite off their fingertips like never before. We now know how many double plays in a game and all that other stuff whereas when I was growing up all we focused on was runs, hits, and errors. Just like in baseball—we don't want to fail today and so the accountant who doesn't deliver this whole array of tools and has the right information at the right time is in trouble. —Participant, Atlanta Focus Group

No one wants to be on the wrong side of the technological revolution. Accounting—as it has been taught and practiced—is seen by many as a relic of the pre-information revolution, and so it is not surprising that practicing accountants, knowing what they do now, would pursue a different major if they were starting their education over again.

Accounting Careers Are Less Attractive Financially than Other Careers

Accounting careers are perceived by many professionals and educators to be less attractive than other business careers in three ways:

1. As discussed in Chapter 3, starting salaries are lower.

2. Independence rules, the requirement to act as partnerships, and other regulations are restricting the ability to accumulate the degree of wealth that is available to other business professionals.

3. The perception is that accounting offers a more limited career track. There was a time when accounting graduates could become the chief executives of their companies because of their understanding of the company as a whole and their understanding of the importance of return-to-investors. That perspective is no longer the exclusive property of accountants and, today, corporate value creation is considered to be more a factor of strategic thinking than anything else.

The problem of starting salaries was addressed in Chapter 2. The independence and other wealth accumulation inhibitions are expressed well by the following *Business Week* quote:

Competition from Wall Street and Silicon Valley, where the rewards can be much richer, plays a big part [in the shortage problem]. Big 5 accountants have just the expertise they need: they know financial accounting, they're technologically savvy, and they have had a broad experience in a wide variety of businesses. But also to blame, many are beginning to argue, are regulations that govern an auditor's ability to invest in stocks.3

There is Less Psychic Income from Being an Accountant than There Used to Be and the CPA Brand is Not Worth What It Was Previously

In two of our four focus groups, professional accountants made comments such as "the psychic income from being a partner in a CPA firm isn't as high as it used to be" and "the CPA brand isn't worth what it used to be." Decreasing numbers of first-time candidates sitting for the CPA exam and the movement of public accounting firms away from being CPA firms to professional service firms tells us a great deal about the value of the CPA brand in the marketplace. The following quote typifies this concern:

Many CPAs currently perceive the opportunities in public accounting to be changing, with less perceived gain for continued demands and commitment. Many CPAs note that the traditional path within a public accounting firm—making partner—is changing, and note greater lengths of time currently necessary to achieve partner. —CPA Vision Project

On the other hand, management accountants—at least those who have successfully transitioned themselves as finance professionals—do not seem to have suffered a similar loss in psychic income. According to the IMA's most recent study *Counting More, Counting Less*, the results show an escalating change in the work performed by management accountants in their role in the organization, and in the value they bring to business decision making.

We asked respondents to rank career choices according to their relative attractiveness. The results found in the table on the following page support the general inclination away from traditional accounting and auditing careers that we heard in our focus group discussions. These results are discouraging to those who are responsible for recruiting for audit and tax functions in CPA firms. They are even more discouraging for those who must recruit into internal audit and government positions.

Consulting work, in any setting, and working in the accounting/finance area of a business organization are perceived as the most challenging and rewarding careers. These results provide some explanation why faculty and practitioners would not pursue an accounting degree today. *Still, these data show that all types of accounting careers are perceived quite positively, a fact that leads us to believe that our respondents' overall disinclination to pursue an accounting education is*

---

3 "Where Have All the Accountants Gone?" *Business Week* 2000.

motivated more by the perceived problems in accounting education than by perceived problems in professional work.

Question Asked	Faculty Who Strongly or Somewhat Disagreed	Faculty Who Strongly or Somewhat Agreed	Practitioners Who Strongly or Somewhat Disagreed	Practitioners Who Strongly or Somewhat Agreed
Working in the consulting area of a CPA firm is a challenging and rewarding career	0.7%%	92.5%	1.2%	88.6%
Working for a consulting firm is a challenging and rewarding career	0.0%	89.9	2.3	86.7
Working in the accounting/finance area of a business organization is a challenging and rewarding career	1.4	92.9	7.2	82.6
Working in the tax area of a CPA firm is a challenging and rewarding career	7.5	72.7	16.4	62.1
Working in the audit/assurance services area of a CPA firm is a challenging and rewarding career	14.2	66.3	19.9	59.1
Working for an investment banking company is a challenging and rewarding career	2.5	66.7	4.3	61.4
Working as a college professor is a challenging and rewarding career	4.3	84.3	14.2	54.9
Working in an internal audit area in a large organization is a challenging and rewarding career	12.5	58.0	39.9	39.3
Working as a governmental accountant is a challenging and rewarding career	32.8	30.2	49.5	25.1

Concluding Remarks

We must all be concerned that both educators and practitioners would choose different majors if starting their education over again today. The perceived low value of an accounting education appears to be caused by two problems: (1) their belief that accounting education does not provide a clear advantage in preparing students to perform the expanding array of services being performed by accountants (or finance professionals) today, and (2) some perceived negative aspects of accounting work that are causing concern among today's accountants.

While both of these reasons were frequently mentioned by focus group participants, we heard more serious concerns about the nature of accounting education. In any event, this is the piece of the problem about which accounting educators can do something. The professional organizations have recognized their own career-image problems, and both the IMA and the AICPA have been working hard to improve the work and image of their members. They must continue, and must further clarify and intensify those campaigns. However, we must not rely on the profession to solve our problems. We have problems with the image and value-added nature of accounting education and we must address these problems ourselves.

CHAPTER 5

Improving Accounting Education

Thus far, we have discussed the bookend problems of decreasing student enrollments and dissatisfaction among graduates. Here we discuss concerns we heard about our educational models. The one message that came across loud and clear in our research, and of which we became convinced, is that most of the educational models we use are "broken" or in desperate need of repair. It many ways, it is not what we have done that has resulted in our current situation as much as it is what we have not done. Accounting education is perceived is having a number of problems, including:

- **Course content and curricula**
- Our curricula are too narrow and often outdated or irrelevant. They are driven by the interests of faculty and not by demands of the market.
- We are not exposing students in the right ways to highly relevant concepts such as globalization, technology, and ethics.
- **Pedagogy**
- Our rule-based, memorization, test-for-content, and prepare-for-certifying-exam educational model is inefficient, but more importantly, it does not prepare students for the ambiguous business world they will encounter upon graduation.
- Our pedagogy often lacks creativity, involves too much lecture and dependence on textbooks, and does not develop the students' ability-to-learn skills. We are too bound by our class time and do not require enough student contact with business.
- **Skill development**
- Our educational models focus too much on content at the expense of skill development—skills our students need to be successful professionals.
- **Technology**
- We teach accounting as if information were still costly. Information is now inexpensive and the part of our curriculum that is devoted to information gathering and recording is a waste of time. Information processing, which has been an important part of our educational model, can now be managed quickly by anyone using the right software.
- Our students are not exposed enough to the impact of technology on business and ways in which technology can be leveraged to make business decisions.
- **Faculty development and reward systems**
- Accounting faculty are often isolated from business-school peers and from business professionals. As a result, we are becoming increasingly out of touch with market and competitive expectations.
- **Strategic direction**
- While a few schools have made good progress in the past few years, changes have not been substantive or pervasive enough and some of the changes that have been made are in the wrong direction. As a result, differences in quality between schools are increasing.
- Because of accounting education's lack of leadership and direction, competition in education has increased, resulting in fewer resources for accounting programs.

We have heard these criticisms before, but never with such collective force. Individually, they might be ignored or dealt with on a piecemeal basis. Taken together, they provide a clarion call for a dramatic change in direction. Our situation is not unlike that of the Titanic. We are being warned that there are icebergs ahead. We can do as the captain of that ship did and push full-steam ahead or we can work hard to improve the educational product we deliver. The several studies of accounting education, beginning with the Bedford Report in 1986, have warned us that changes were needed. While some educators have heeded previous warnings and made changes, we have not done enough. As one educator said:

> *We've been revising the curriculum significantly over the last several years, trying to react to the marketplace demands. Now we are beginning to realize that the changes needed may be significantly more than previously anticipated.* —Participant, AICPA Vision Focus Group

In this chapter, we will discuss perceived problems with accounting education. We will begin by making three general observations, followed by a discussion of content, pedagogy, skill development, technology, curricular, and strategy issues.

General Observations about Accounting Education

Observation #1—Some Schools Have Changed

It is obvious that a few schools have heeded the call for change and have tried hard to keep up with changes in the business world. However, it is just as obvious that even these changes have not been pervasive or substantive enough. The result of these changes, however, are increasingly larger differences in quality between accounting programs. The following comments illustrate this observation.

> *I think a lot of the changes being made in accounting education today are piecemeal. It's a start and that's important. But, I think that a lot of us feel that it's not moving fast enough and it's not pervasive enough to really provide as many graduates that are more broadly educated and have the backgrounds that we need. Some of the programs that were involved in the Accounting Education Change Commission have made very pervasive changes. They went through and looked at their entire programs and integrated all the way through the fifth year. That's a lot of what we like to see happen.* —Participant, New York Focus Group

> *What I see, because I go to so many schools, is that there are different programs in place at each school and every student is going through a different type of education. Some of the basic accounting stuff may be there, but the advanced-level stuff or some of the things that bring it home—you know, the school activities—those vary widely by college. So, if you recruit students from a lot of schools like I do, you're going to see that some have good experiences that their school provides for them and others don't. And, when you put them together, you notice the differences right away.* —Participant, New York Focus Group

Unfortunately, the perceptions expressed in these quotes suggest a scattershot approach by schools and faculty. This conclusion has support in the responses we received to our survey. To understand what has been taking place in accounting education, we asked department chairs to describe the changes that have been made to their undergraduate and graduate programs during the past ten years. Their responses begin on the next page.

Question Asked— Undergraduate Accounting Programs	Percent of Department Chairs Who Stated That This Response Best Describes the Changes They Have Made	Percent of Department Chairs Who Stated That This Response Next Best Describes the Changes They Have Made
Have combined our accounting major with another business major such as finance or information systems	5.7	11.2
Have totally revised our accounting major curriculum and/or requirements	24.6	14.3
Have added several new classes and updated as needed for technical content changes but still have basically the same accounting curriculum we had ten years ago	39.3	26.5
Have not added or deleted many classes but have made substantial changes to the pedagogy of existing classes as well as updating as needed for technical content changes	24.6	39.8
Course content, pedagogy, and classes are the same as those of ten years ago	5.8	8.2

Question Asked	Percent of Department Chairs Who Stated That This Response Describes Changes They Have Made to Their Undergraduate Accounting Programs	Percent of Department Chairs Who Stated That This Response Describes Changes They Have Made to Their Graduate Accounting Programs
Have added skills-development components to most of our accounting classes	64.9	41.0
Have added technology components to most of our accounting classes	73.1	47.8
Have added requirements that students visit and/or interact with business professionals and/or firms to most of our accounting classes	20.9	15.7
Have added group-work components to most of our accounting classes	67.9	43.3
Have added service-learning assignments to most of our accounting classes	7.5	6.0

While these changes are on target, on the whole, they are inadequate. Very few successful businesses would report that they were working with substantially the same product they had ten years ago. Few would admit that, in the last ten years, they had only worked technology into 47.8 percent of their activities. When we asked department chairs to compare their 1990 and 2000 course catalogues and identify specific courses that have been added or dropped, we were disappointed with the types of changes described. While we admit that it is difficult to assess degree of change from the response to a one- or two-sentence question, it appears that many of the changes made have merely added more in-depth coverage of various accounting topics. Further, it appears that the changes have been made in response to interests of the faculty rather than to market demands. Here are the specific courses that have been added or dropped from curricula of respondents. In many cases, there were several schools that added or dropped the same course.

Undergraduate Courses

Content-Type Courses Added to Undergraduate Program	Broadening-Type Courses Added to Undergraduate Program	Content-Type Courses Dropped from Undergraduate Program	Broadening-Type Courses Dropped from Undergraduate Program
Advanced managerial accounting	Tax research	Financial accounting theory	Introduction to accounting— survey course
Advanced tax	Financial statement analysis	Not-for-profit	Estate and gift tax research
Not-for-profit accounting	First-year course on core concepts	International accounting	Governmental
Accounting theory	Accounting information systems	Advanced accounting	Computerized accounting
Advanced accounting	Enterprise systems and business process analysis	Federal tax III	Financial statement analysis
Controllership	Financial management for nonmajors	CPA Review	
Advanced cost accounting	Accounting technology and computer applications	Third auditing class— EDP auditing	
Intermediate financial III	EDP auditing	Advanced cost accounting	
EDP Computer Auditing	Financial accounting research	Intermediate accounting II	
Accounting for quality		Controllership	
Cash management	International accounting and finance	Electronic spreadsheets	
Accounting history	Competitive strategy using accounting information	Governmental accounting	
Governmental auditing	Advanced written communications and presentation	Regulatory accounting	
Estate and gift taxes	Personal finance	Advanced tax	
Advanced budgeting		Business law II	
Advanced auditing		Intermediate II	
Financial for nonmajors		EDP auditing	
Managerial for nonmajors		Partnership and fund accounting	
Tax accounting II		Accounting theory	
Internal auditing		Third auditing class	
Governmental accounting		Introduction to accounting	
International accounting		Software for small businesses	
Accounting theory		Estate and gift taxes	
International accounting		Oil and gas accounting	

Graduate Courses

Content-Type Courses Added to Graduate Program	Broadening-Type Courses Added to Graduate Program	Content-Type Courses Dropped from Graduate Program	Broadening-Type Courses Dropped from Graduate Program
Auditing theory	Database management, networks and JAVA	Oil and gas taxation	Professional conduct and ethics
Capstone accounting course	Shareholder value creation	Advanced managerial accounting	Contemporary issues in accounting
Tax III	Accounting for e-commerce	Advanced auditing	
Comparative accounting theory	Tax Research	CPA review	
EVA	Communications	Governmental accounting	
Advanced accounting II	Financial statement analysis	Accounting theory	
Advanced managerial accounting	Computer applications	Budgeting and control systems	
Tax practicum	ERP	Estate and gift taxes	
Oil and gas accounting	Risk analysis and control	Partnerships and S-Corps	
Advanced accounting I	Accounting services marketing	Accountametrics	
International accounting	Computer and operational auditing	Advanced tax and tax planning	
International and multijurisdictional taxation	Business consulting	Management accounting in textiles and manufacturing	
Operational auditing	Forensic accounting	Internal auditing	
Strategic cost management	Financial statement analysis	Computer auditing	
Advanced budgeting	Organizations and society	Oil and gas tax policy	
Governmental accounting	Joint IS/Acctg. Program	Public utility accounting	
History of accounting	Research methodology		
Accounting theory	Valuation, mergers and acquisitions		
Tax policy	Ethics in tax		
Advanced auditing			
Financial accounting for nonmajors			
Managerial accounting for nonmajors			
Corporate financial reporting			

While the list on the preceding page identifies only the names of classes added or dropped, *there were significantly more classes added than dropped.* Consistent with the responses to the earlier questions about curricula changes, it appears that we are working around the edges, adding more similar classes, rather than making substantive changes to our curricula.

Observation #2—Competition Has Arrived

A second observation is that increased competition has come to accounting education. For years, public and not-for-profit private universities have had a monopoly on higher education. Within that educational setting, accounting programs have had a monopoly on educating students to become professional accountants in industry and public accounting. Firms that wanted to hire accountants focused their recruiting activities on traditional college campuses and accounting programs. These educational and hiring monopolies no longer exist. Two major types of competition have arrived. The first is competition from other business and nonbusiness disciplines. As the work our graduates perform has changed, other majors such as finance, information systems, computer science, logistics, strategy, and even the generalized M.B.A., have become increasingly attractive to recruiters. We have lost our monopoly on providing students who become professional accountants.

In addition, the popularity of business school, especially M.B.A., rankings has resulted in a transfer of resources away from accounting programs to other business programs. As deans and other school administrators have scurried to improve their M.B.A. rankings, they have directed more resources toward M.B.A. programs. It is obvious from our department-chair survey that accounting administrators are witnessing this shifting of resources. When we asked them to think about the money, faculty, and other resources that their universities allocate to the various business-school programs and how their accounting resources stacked up against other programs, they responded that the relative percentage of resources allocated to accounting programs has:

Response	Percent of Department Chairs Who Responded
Increased relative to other business programs	5.7
Stayed about the same relative to other business programs	32.5
Decreased relative to other business programs	61.8

When we asked chairs whose resources had decreased relative to other business programs to rank-order the most important reasons for the decreases, respondents ranked reasons in the following order:

1. Other existing programs, such as information systems and logistics/supply-chain management, have taken resources from accounting.

2. The M.B.A. rankings in business periodicals have diverted resources away from other business-school programs toward M.B.A. programs.

3. We have fewer students in accounting than we did previously.

4. Accounting is not perceived as important a discipline at our school as it was previously.

5. Resources at our school have decreased and everyone now has fewer resources than before.

These results emphasize the point made earlier—that we are losing students to other, more attractive business and related programs and that these other programs are being rewarded with larger budgets.

The second type of competition is the proliferation of for-profit universities, such as the DeVry Institute of Technology and the University of Phoenix, and from distance-learning programs. These types of schools are now among the largest private universities in the U.S., based on enrollment. During the past five years, more than 1,000 for-profit universities have begun operations, some of which are now actively seeking approval by accreditation bodies, or partnering with accredited traditional universities. One 1998 survey, for example, found that 40 percent of for-profit universities plan to grant degrees in partnership with accredited institutions of higher education. Recent *Wall*

Street Journal articles addressed this new kind of competition. Consider the following quotes from those articles:

Perhaps nowhere is the pinch between the old way of doing business and the new being felt more acutely than in the very birthplace of the Internet: the hallowed halls of academia. Some $6 billion in venture capital has flowed into the education sector since 1990—almost half of it since last year, when Cisco Systems Inc.'s John Chambers dubbed eduation "the next big killer application on the Internet." Analysts expect new investment of $4 billion in the sector this year. From notHarvard.com to UniversityAccess.com to Medschool.com, the Internet landscape is now dotted with learning ventures offering everything from corporate training to software designed to improve the ways schools run to long-distance learning. With so many entrepreneurs out to chip away at their brick-and-mortal souls, colleges and universities of all stripes are defending their turf—and what analysts estimate to be a $250 billion market. —Ann Grimes

Media financier Herbert Allen, Jr. wants to bring some show-business magic to one of the Internet's biggest and most controversial potential markets: beaming classes from top-notch colleges to vast numbers of students via the Web. Mr. Allen is the prime backer of Global Education Network, a start-up that has been quietly working over the past year and a half to bring Ivy League universities and other top-tier liberal-arts colleges together in a consortium to provide online education. "If we're right, we will create a product that will challenge the product being generated in their classrooms," said Mr. Allen. To do that, he has infused the endeavor with a media-savvy sensibility. Programmers and film crews are already busy assembling a slate of "beta" courses, creating computer graphics and taping lectures on several campuses, with plans to begin rolling out a test version of the service by the end of the year. —Thomas E. Weber

Distance programs may be the least costly and most efficient of all educational delivery systems and can be provided to large numbers of students almost as inexpensively as they can to a few students. The fact that these programs are going head-to-head with traditional universities is obvious from the mission statement of the Western Governors University, which reads:

The principal mission of Western Governors University is to improve quality and expand access to post-secondary educational opportunities by providing a means for individuals to learn, independent of time or place, and to earn competency-based degrees and other credentials that are credible to both academic institutions and employers.

These competitors intensify the need for traditional accounting programs to distinguish themselves in unique ways. Failure to do so will result in these lower-cost alternatives causing the decline in our enrollments to accelerate.

Observation #3—The Most Critical Element in a Student's Successful Classroom Experience is an Inspiring Professor

A third observation is, regardless of curricular and other changes made, an effective and inspiring teacher makes more difference to a student's educational experience than any other factor. When we asked focus-group participants why they studied accounting and what they liked most about their accounting education, the answer was always the same—it was an inspiring and passionate professor who made the difference. The following quotes are typical of the comments we heard most frequently.

My favorite class was my tax class. My professor was energetic, he made the class think about the class, and forced us to use our brains as to why things are the way they are. And he would just sit there and watch you think. If you were trying to figure out what was going on, he was patient. And in his tax course, you were overly confused, but he would just help you along—he'd never give you the answers. He was very passionate. And, when the class was over, he had chalk all over his arms, all over his shirt because he was so excited about teaching the course. —Participant, Los Angeles Focus Group

The best experience I had was a teacher that I had in advanced accounting. I was competing with a lot of World War II veterans and they were highly motivated. I had this teacher—we called her

*Mad Mary—but she really stretched us. That is the sign of a good teacher, not just one that gives a test and didactic type of teaching, but one who really stretched the students—and she did that in advanced accounting. Nobody could think that mergers and acquisitions could be that exciting, but she managed to pound it into us and you know, made us work. —*Participant, Los Angeles Focus Group

*The class I got the most out of was an audit class. It was really different. We did a real audit and worked in a team environment. You had an end product at the end of the class that you presented to the rest of the people in the class. There was a very passionate teacher—he had real-life experience that he could bring to the class and really helped open up a lot of possibilities in the auditing field that I hadn't known. —*Participant, Los Angeles Focus Group

Perceived Problems with Accounting Education

The practice community believes that accounting education has serious problems. While the practice world is not above criticism, that is not the purpose of this study. As a result of completing this study, we have come to the conclusion that the problems our constituents have identified need to be addressed seriously. There is hope. The first step in solving the problems is to understand clearly what critics are trying to tell us. We wish you could have walked in our shoes during the past eight months. Our experiences during that time have convinced us that if serious changes are not made, accounting education will lose its relevance to our business schools, to our students, and to the employers who might otherwise be interested in our students.

There are six major categories of perceived problems: (1) course content and curriculum, (2) pedagogy, (3) skill development, (4) use of technology, (5) faculty development and reward structures, and (6) strategic planning and direction of accounting programs and departments. We will address each of these.

Problems with Our Course Content and Curriculum

Critics argue that our course content and curriculum needs a complete overhaul. They contend that the minor tinkering we have been doing by adding assignments to selected classes or adding a few new classes has not been sufficient. Think about the traditional course requirements for an accounting major:

* An introductory accounting course where debits and credits are taught and where financial statement preparation is emphasized.
* An introductory managerial course that teaches cost accumulation and the preparation of budgets
* One or more intermediate courses—or should we call them "financial accounting fast"—where the students study detailed rules and pronouncements related to financial statement line items.
* Cost accounting—or should we call it "managerial accounting fast"—that reinforces and goes into more detail on the topics covered in introductory managerial accounting.
* Several specific auditing and tax courses where students cover detailed auditing standards and IRS rulings.

While this traditional program may create a good accountant, the business world has told us that they want a good businessperson. As one interviewee stated, "the practice profession has been highly innovative while accounting education has not. What we teach no longer matches what the core competencies of the profession are." Our focus-group participants told us they appreciated the rigor of our courses, and feel the overall view instilled by an accounting education is invaluable. However, they urged us to cover the basics quickly and avoid the temptation to increase curricula with follow-on courses refining the basics and studying details in more depth. After one focus-group participant suggested that we stop after one intermediate class, there was clear consensus in support of that view. One respected professor expressed this concern well when he said:

Our courses are too detailed and too technical, especially intermediate and cost accounting. We need to admit that we were wrong in our curriculum decisions.

Our insistence on covering topics in so much detail has led to many criticisms regarding accounting curricula and course content. Some of the most frequent criticisms are:

1. Our courses are too often taught as a series of technical rules, resulting in a conformance orientation.

2. Our curricula and content are too focused on professional examinations and achieving the right answer.

3. Our curricula are too narrow, do not expose students to a broad business education, and do not use enough real-world examples.

4. We do not use a global perspective to teach accounting.

5. We do not deal enough with values, ethics, and integrity.

6. We teach too much of what accountants used to do instead of what they will do.

7. We have developed 150-hour programs that require students to take additional content-based courses rather than learning critical skills that will make them successful.

8. Our Ph.D. programs, which are designed primarily to help faculty develop narrow research agendas, perpetuate the focus on detailed specialization which carries into classrooms.

9. Our introductory accounting classes give students the wrong impression of what accountants do. For the most part, they perpetuate the bookkeeping and rule-based orientation students were exposed to in high school.

10. We do not teach students how technology has reshaped everything we do in business. Rather, we assume we have adequately covered technology when we give them spreadsheet and database assignments.

The following quotes highlight some of these criticisms.

The tremendous benefit that comes out of an accounting education is the organization and the structure and the discipline and the understanding you gain from looking at the business from an accountant's eyes. But then the course goes off into a study of paragraph 114 of SFAS 131, and all that perspective is lost. —Interviewee

New graduates don't know anything about business. Now, that's a broad, sweeping, generalist kind of statement, but they don't understand manufacturing. They don't understand distribution. They don't understand banking. They don't understand insurance. And yet, they get thrown right into, in some cases, very large organizations, in some cases small organizations, and they don't seem to have a grasp of what a business does. —Participant, Chicago Focus Group

I've found that I'd never had any hands-on stuff in school—you only get that in the internship you go to during the summer. Other than that, you get zero hands on, it's all textbook. You get out in the real world, and in these last six months, I've found it's not textbook. It's very much looking at things and seeing how the numbers interact with each other and seeing that relationship that no one helped me understand in school. —Participant (recent college graduate), Chicago Focus Group

Students need to be exposed to ethical issues and dilemmas. We had an experience this summer where we had an intern with us—an individual from a big university. He took it upon himself not only to pad his expense report, but to teach the other interns how to do it. Initiative? We terminated that individual in the middle of the internship and explained to the university what was going on. Somewhere in the university, students have got to get ethics training. —Participant, Chicago Focus Group

To help us assess which topics (content knowledge) are most important, we asked respondents to our survey to rank various topics as 1 (not important), 2 (somewhat important—part of a course), 3 (moderately important—one college course), or 4 (very important—more than one course). The following are the results:

Topic	Average Faculty Rank	Average Practitioner Rank
Financial accounting	3.74	3.57
Information systems	3.54	3.56
Finance	3.36	3.28
Taxes	3.30	3.28
Managerial accounting	3.25	3.05
Auditing/assurance services	3.13	3.06
Economics	3.10	2.81
Technology topics	3.08	3.01
Statistics/quantitative methods	3.00	2.73
Business strategy	2.91	3.15
Business law	2.84	2.95
Global/international business	2.80	2.92
E-commerce	2.77	3.00
Marketing	2.63	2.45
Organizational behavior/human resources	2.60	2.46
Ethics	2.54	2.89
Operations/supply-chain management	2.51	2.48
Accounting research methods	2.13	2.50

It is interesting to note that there are seven topics that practitioners felt were more important than educators: information systems, business strategy, business law, global/international business, e-commerce, ethics, and accounting research methods. These are generally broadening-type courses. Courses traditionally included in accounting programs were ranked higher by educators than by practitioners.

In our focus groups, we heard many complaints about five-year programs; most were criticisms about the way these programs have been developed. Practitioners are very concerned that we have just added "more of the same." Consider the following comment.

> *The 150-hour rule is about not only what we are going to add on, but about how we should approach the students' entire education so that we can make it integrated and stop teaching those things that are no longer relevant. We need to teach them in a different way and look at it as a whole program rather than just an add-on. Too many of the 150-hour programs merely added on more accounting at the fifth year and that's not what we wanted.* —Participant, New York Focus Group

> *The five-year accounting degree continues to be a challenge, especially due to a lack of reward (differential salary) compared to other options. It is genuinely difficult to advise students to choose the Master's of Accountancy degree over other options.* —Comment on accounting educator questionnaire

To help us assess the validity of these criticisms, we asked department chairs about the nature of their fifth-year programs. We first asked how many had five-year programs and then asked about those programs. Here is what we found when we asked which response best describes the status of their graduate programs in accounting ten years ago and today.

Response	Percent of Department Chairs Who Chose This Response
We didn't have a master's degree program in accounting ten years ago and we still don't have one today.	8.0
We have added a new master's degree program during the past ten years to comply with the 150-hour requirement to sit for the CPA exam to become a CPA.	31.8
We had a master's degree in accounting ten years ago but we have substantially revised the degree requirements during the past ten years.	47.7
We had a master's degree in accounting ten years ago and we have basically the same degree requirements today as we had then.	12.5

Ninety-two percent of respondents offer master's degree programs in accounting. Because we wanted to assess whether the "add-on" criticism was valid, we asked department chairs which of the following responses best describes the nature of their fifth year required to complete the master's degree program at their schools. Here are their responses.

Response	Percent of Department Chairs Who Chose This Response
The fifth year is comprised mostly of accounting courses that help students specialize in an area of concentration, such as tax, assurance services, managerial accounting, etc.	27.2
The fifth year is comprised mostly of courses that are intended to provide students with a broad background in business, such as additional finance, marketing, technology, and communication courses.	7.4
The fifth year is comprised of approximately an equal mix of broad-based and specialty courses.	65.4

While the widespread notion that the fifth year has suffered from add-on accounting courses may be overstated, it is obvious from these data that there have been many specialty courses added. There also appears to have been some broad business courses added. Still, very few schools have effectively built their undergraduate degree with a fifth year that focuses on providing a broad business background.

It may be that we have taken exactly the wrong approach in developing our fifth-year programs. Instead of adding almost exclusively broadening-type experiences and courses, as those who developed the law envisioned, we have added too many additional accounting courses. Because we have a certain kind of training (and tenure), we have used our training to add additional courses that we can teach. The result has been more courses that we can teach without retooling, but narrower and more specialized programs for our students. These specialized programs are not attractive in an environment where the business world is calling for broadly trained accountants.

Problems with Pedagogy

How would you feel if you received personal student-teacher evaluations that not only told you your course content was irrelevant, but also that the way you delivered that content was flawed? That is essentially what critics, including focus-group participants and survey respondents, told us. Here is what they say is wrong with our pedagogy.

1. There is too much emphasis on memorization. Our tests are based primarily on recall. One participant referred to our emphasis on memorization and regurgitate as the "trained-monkey" approach.

2. There is too much lecture, reliance on textbooks as course drivers, and "faculty knows best" attitude.

3. We are reluctant to develop creative types of learning, such as team work, assignments with real companies, case analysis, oral presentations, role playing, team teaching, technology assignments, videos, writing assignments, involving business professionals in the classroom, and studying current events.

4. We do not use enough out-of-classroom experiences, such as internships, field studies, foreign business trips, online (Internet) experiences, service-learning assignments, and shadowing of professionals.

The following comments by focus group participants are representative of these pedagogical criticisms.

I don't think the purpose of education is to teach specific content. I think it's to teach students how to think and how to navigate their way through new experiences so that they will have a context or a framework to work from that they will understand and pick things up quickly. So the more rich contacts that we can give them in the educational experience, the more we challenge them to think for themselves, the better. We need to get more consistency across different curriculums around the country to challenge students to really be able to think and not just come up with problems and answers. Unfortunately, my education was very much memorize and regurgitate. —Participant, Chicago Focus Group

I look back on my auditing class and I can still remember having to memorize an unqualified report. I had to memorize that and then on the test, I had to write it out. Why in the heck did I ever have to do that? Yeah, you've got to know the basic three paragraphs or whatever, but now I just go to my technical book. Why did I have to memorize that? How much time that took was unbelievable. —Participant, Chicago Focus Group

These pedagogy problems are not unique to accounting education. However, the combination of technology replacing much of what we have traditionally covered and the proliferation of standards that make research skills more valuable than memorization of facts, exacerbate the problem in accounting. We can argue that finance and information systems professors have the same problems, but their curricula have generally not been as content-specific as ours, allowing them to avoid the same imperative for pedagogical change we feel.

To assess faculty use and feelings about various pedagogical approaches, we asked educators about which learning activities they use and believe are most effective. Here is what we found:

Learning Activity	Percent Who Currently Use	Percent Who Do Not Use	Percent Who Believe Not Useful and Should Not Be Used	Percent Who Believe but Used Too Much	Perecent Who Believe Useful and Used About Right	Percent Who Believe Useful and Should Be Used More
Assignments with real companies	40.8	59.2	5.1	4.3	37.9	52.7
Case analysis	69.3	30.7	2.7	8.5	51.3	37.5
Feedback exercises (quizzes, etc.)	75.6	24.4	4.3	10.5	73.5	11.7
Lecture	90.6	9.4	0.8	41.4	56.3	1.5
Oral presentations	62.4	37.6	4.0	8.4	53.3	34.3
Reading textbooks	84.0	16.0	6.3	12.1	73.8	7.8
Role playing	15.3	84.7	39.3	5.2	21.4	34.1
Team (group) work	74.6	25.4	3.1	20.4	48.7	27.8
Team teaching	11.1	88.9	26.0	4.3	21.2	48.5
Technology assignments	77.0	23.0	2.4	5.1	39.5	53.0
Videos	37.6	62.4	22.5	5.4	59.2	12.9
Writing assignments	78.4	21.6	1.6	2.4	50.2	45.8

A review of these data suggest we know what needs to be done—it also suggests we have not done it. Why, if we believe there is too much lecture, do we continue to rely on it? Why, if we believe it would be profitable to develop assignments with real companies, is it not done more? You can ask the same questions about team teaching and technology assignments. Faculty seem to know what to do, but do not do it.

We also asked practitioners and educators how strongly they felt about various out-of-classroom learning activities. When we asked them to allocate 20 points among the following learning activities (the more points allocated, the more useful they felt the activity was), we found the following:

Learning Activity	Number of Faculty Allocating Points to This Activity	Average Points Allocated by Faculty	Number of Practitioners Allocating Points to This Activity	Average Points Allocated by Practitioners
3–4 month internships with companies	267	9.29	465	8.63
Field study projects with real companies	229	4.54	384	4.42
Service learning assignments	196	3.53	356	4.26
Shadowing professionals	154	2.63	341	3.33
Foreign business trips	138	2.70	246	1.77
Online (Internet) classes	121	2.47	283	2.33

Not surprisingly, practitioners and faculty believe an internship is the best out-of-classroom learning activity. However, also we heard frequently that, to be effective, an internship needs to be carefully managed by both the school and the firm. An effective internship is not just temporary employment, but also it must be a learning experience. There must be ongoing faculty monitoring of the experience and the students must know that they will be evaluated by the school and the firm. Service-learning assignments also scored high, especially among educators. Field studies received significant points, while shadowing professionals, foreign business trips, and online experiences were allocated fewer points by fewer respondents.

Lack of Skill Development

Students forget what they memorize. Content knowledge becomes dated and is often not transferable across different types of jobs. On the other hand, critical skills rarely become obsolete and are usually transferable across assignments and careers. Accounting education has frequently been criticized for spending too much time on content mastery and too little time and effort to helping students to develop skills that will enrich their lives and make them successful. The following comments are typical of these criticisms.

The analytical ability of auditors, particularly young auditors, is atrocious. They don't understand financial statement analysis. And, when they do find something that deviates from their expectations, they don't have the confidence to pursue the questions. —Interviewee

We have not trained our students in accounting to deal with uncertainty. Most of them say, "I've got to get my spreadsheet complete before I can make a decision." But today, you have to make some decisions with some risk. You have got to be able to make a decision without perfect knowledge. I think we should look at how we teach people and we should give them some more cases with uncertainty. —Participant, Los Angeles Focus Group

I think of the way that communication has changed because of the Internet, email, voice mail. A lot of the time you don't even have face time with people anymore. The students we're seeing right now, they're a dot.com generation. They're a generation that grew up with that as opposed to all of us and they're used to just shooting a quick email and not going in depth or having the face time with someone. So I think the way communication has changed in general affects everyone, but going back to my students, they really are different. They are a dot.com technology generation and they're lacking in some of the different types of communication styles that we were all used to. — Participant, New York Focus Group

To assess which skills educators and practitioners believe are most important, we asked respondents to prioritize skills in terms of how much class time should be spent developing each. On a scale of 1 (no priority) to 5 (top priority), they ranked skills as follows:

Skill	Average Faculty Ranking	Average Practitioner Ranking
Analytical/critical thinking	4.53	4.29
Written communications	4.39	4.32
Oral communications	4.22	4.27
Computing technology	4.10	4.07
Decision making	4.03	3.96
Interpersonal skills	3.94	3.89
Continuous learning	3.82	3.70
Teamwork	3.81	4.02
Business decision modeling	3.65	3.65
Professional demeanor	3.64	3.66
Leadership	3.58	3.83
Risk analysis	342	3.39
Measurement	3.36	3.12
Project management	3.26	3.66
Customer orientation	3.23	3.34
Change management	3.13	3.36
Negotiation	3.13	3.35
Research	3.08	3.26
Entrepreneurship	2.99	3.24
Resource management	2.98	3.32
Salesmanship	2.61	2.79
Foreign language	2.60	2.56

Interestingly, faculty and practice respondents were in substantial agreement as to which are the most important skills. It is also important to recognize that this ranking of skills aligns closely with the core competencies identified in the AICPA Vision Study and its Core Competency Framework for entry-level students, by the IMA in their 1995 and 1999 Practice Analyses, by the Institute of Internal Auditors in their recent study of the knowledge base of internal auditing, by the AECC, and with academic research on accounting education. It is interesting to note that faculty feel more strongly than do practitioners about the higher-ranking skills, but less strongly than do practitioners on most of the lower-ranking skills. Using 3 as a cutoff, there are only two skills that practitioners believe should have little or no priority. If we effectively teach these skills, we will add value that cannot be duplicated through distance learning and other lower-cost delivery methods. We must find ways to integrate the teaching of skills into our curricula.

Failure to Exploit Technology

We understand the need to use technology in our teaching and to expose students to technology. However, do we understand what is meant when we say students need to learn technology? We are not sure we understood when we began this study. Our initial thoughts were that technology meant using various technology tools to solve problems, understanding systems controls and maybe some programming, and understanding technology terminology. While understanding these aspects of technology are important, probably even more critical is understanding how technology has re-shaped everything we do. Students need to understand how technology has made information cheaper, for example. As professors, we need to know what cheap information means for the way we teach.

Students need to know what cheap information means for the work they will perform as professionals. It also means they need to know how technology is used to facilitate and drive business, including everything from communication, to on-demand information for decision making, and to the importance of strategic partnerships. Technology has revolutionized everything, including the way we live and work. It should have caused us to completely rethink everything we teach, not just whether we should add an Internet or spreadsheet assignment. Technology has made business models and transactions more complex, has shortened product life cycles, and has been the enabler for dynamic change in the business community. It has created a demand for instant feedback and instant answers. Our students must understand how technology has and will continue to change the way we provide and use information to make decisions. Critics argue that many educators have still not caught the vision of what this means.

While we did not ask questions in our surveys about the impact of technology on business, we did ask participants which technology skills they believed new accounting graduates should have. When we asked them to rank the skill as either a 1 (not important for new hires to possess), 2 (nice to know, but not critical), or 3 (critical), these were their rankings:

Technology Skill	Average Faculty Response	Average Practitioner Response
Spreadsheet software	2.94	2.89
Word-processing software	2.92	2.76
Windows	2.82	2.80
World Wide Web	2.76	2.47
Presentation software	2.64	2.42
Technology terminology	2.60	2.47
Database software	2.59	2.41
Information systems planning and strategy	2.49	2.28
Electronic commerce	2.51	2.28
Technology security and controls	2.50	2.37
File and directory management	2.50	2.42
Communications software (e.g., Outlook)	2.38	2.33
Systems analysis	2.22	2.04
Project management	2.09	2.29
Technology management and budgeting	2.07	2.13
Intra/Extranets	2.06	2.02
Graphics software (e.g., Adobe)	2.03	1.89
Computer hardware	1.99	1.95
Computer operations management	1.98	2.02
HTML and other web programming	1.76	1.60
Other operating systems	1.72	1.83
Programming languages	1.52	1.52

These responses show a high degree of consensus between the importance rankings of educators and practitioners. If we use a cutoff of 2.5 (halfway between "nice to know" and "critical"), faculty believe there are ten and practitioners believe there are three technology skills that absolutely cannot be ignored in our curricula.

Program Issues

Thus far, our discussion has focused on aspects of the educational process over which faculty have significant influence or control—curriculum, course content, pedagogy, skill development, and technology. Now, we turn our attention to criticisms of accounting education that are more departmental or programmatic. Administrators are directly responsible for these program elements.

What if all businesses offered the same products or services in exactly the same way? In addition, what if all those businesses had different raw materials to work with, different amounts of resources to bring to the product-development process, and different marketing outlets? In this world of instantaneously available information, only those entities that wisely exploited their strategic advantages would survive. Is that not the situation accounting education is in? We have numerous schools all trying to prepare students for the same markets with varying amounts of resources and varying quality inputs. Few accounting programs have a distinct personality; most of them are clones of other programs. Many schools have Ph.D. programs that look like all other Ph.D. programs. Many schools focus on teaching to the CPA exam, emphasizing public and financial accounting at the expense of managerial accounting and other career opportunities. Most schools teach a financial-based introductory accounting course.

While this "copycat" strategy has been successful in the past—where supply, capacity, and demand were in equilibrium, and where instantaneously available information did not readily expose schools' weaknesses—it will not work in the future. As stated in Chapter 3, the number of student enrollments is down. With more information available about the strengths and weaknesses of individual schools, and with schools having differing resources, quality of students, and faculty passion, some schools will not be competitive in the future if they do not define a specific strategy that exploits their competitive strengths. Without proactive action by accounting program leaders, we may soon experience the demise of many stand-alone accounting programs. Our accounting faculty will either be terminated or absorbed into other departments. We can stop, or at least slow down, this demise by addressing the issues discussed earlier in this chapter. But, we must do more.

Concluding Comments

Have our criticisms of accounting education been too harsh? Maybe. But then, previous cries of impending danger have been largely ignored. We have spent far too much time resting on our traditions and looking in the rearview mirror when we should have been teaching to the future. With the right direction and work, accounting education has a bright future. That future depends upon the actions we take now.

CHAPTER 6

Summary and Recommendations

In 1978, there was a United Airlines night flight from Denver to Portland. In the cockpit were the pilot, the co-pilot, the flight engineer, the navigator, and a visiting full captain who was "dead heading" (flying along to bring back an empty plane from Portland.) The flight was uneventful until the pilot attempted to put down the landing gear. Failing to get the light indicators that the gear was down, the pilot performed backup procedures. There was still no indication of whether the gear was down. As a last resort, the captain flew by the tower for visual inspection. The tower radioed back that it appeared that the landing gear was down and locked.

Because he was uncertain about the landing gear, the pilot elected to circle around one more time to burn off more fuel. The navigator, flight engineer, and co-pilot counseled against circling again saying the fuel was almost gone. Knowing their voices were being recorded, several crew members stated they had counseled against the go-around decision. The visiting captain said, "I know these DC-8s and one thing I know for sure—they don't fly well without fuel." He then left the cockpit, walked briskly to the last row in the passenger compartment and put his head between his legs and a pillow behind his head for the crash position.

Upon final approach, the plane ran out of fuel, crashed into two large (empty) homes, skidded across a busy street, had its wings sheared off by trees, and broke in half. Miraculously, no one on the ground was killed and only 12 passengers and one flight attendant died (all in first class.) At the inquiry associated with the civil suits against the pilot and the airlines, the flight transcripts were read. For the first time in history, the Airline Pilots Association (APA) declined to support the pilot. Their position was that when the pilot decided to go alone and ignore all the collective wisdom that he heard that night, he decided to go alone in court.[1]

As accounting educators, we must not emulate the United Airlines pilot and ignore the warnings from our colleagues and the evidence at hand. We can no longer deny that there are serious problems with accounting education. We have an enterprise that is experiencing decreased customer demand, where past customers are recommending that prospective customers shop elsewhere, and where there are significant complaints about our services and products. Accounting education is in a precarious condition.

Frankly, whether accounting programs survive as currently structured probably is not all that important. What matters is that we determine how to add high value to our students as they prepare for careers in a fast-changing business world. We have the capability to do that, but we need to step outside our comfort zone, stretch ourselves, and begin to teach and research in new areas. We

---

[1] The story of this incident was recorded by one of the founders of Franklin-Covey, who was supposedly told the story by one of the pilots on board the crashed airplane.

understand measurement and we teach it well. We need to help business and our students develop new, more relevant measures of performance. We understand information systems and we excel in teaching the oldest and most established information system. We need to move beyond financial accounting and help business and our students to develop the information systems they need to make critical, strategic decisions. We understand financial analysis because we know where the numbers come from. We need to move beyond the gathering of the data and help businesses and our students to develop new ways of interpreting and using their data. Those expanded opportunities are ours to lose.

We could sit back and hope salaries for our graduates will increase substantially and students will come flocking back to our classes and programs. However, we do not believe, as some of the respondents to surveys have suggested, that our problems are only a function of salaries. There may very well be a stronger relationship between the "value add" of an accounting education and the starting salaries of our graduates than we are willing to admit. Perhaps programs based on obsolete assumptions such as "information is expensive to produce," "a narrow but deep education is better than a broad-based education," and "it is more important to teach content than skills" are not adding as much value as we think they are. After our work on this project, we have come to believe that the decisions we will make, as accounting educators, in the next few years are more important than any we have made in the past.

How We Would Structure Future Accounting Programs

The four organizations sponsoring this study asked us to conclude our "thought piece" with recommendations of what we would do to remedy perceived problems in accounting education. Their request asked us to be bold, forward-thinking, and hold nothing back.

We are happy to share our thoughts and observations based on our research, hoping they will stimulate discussion and follow-up action. The recommendations we will provide below are based on three primary observations:

1. The AACSB was absolutely right when it concluded that each school or department must decide for itself what its mission is, and then establish a strategic plan to achieve that mission. We need to accept that philosophy and implement it, both in fact and in spirit. Many of our focus-group participants bemoaned the prevalence of the cookie-cutter approach we have followed in developing accounting curricula. One interviewee expressed the problem quite succinctly when he said:

   > We have been following "a one shoe fits all" approach to curricula, to teaching, to students, and to faculty development.

   There is no one model or prescription that all schools should adopt to resolve the crisis we face in accounting education. Faculty in each department must decide for themselves what their response will be.[2]

2. It is critical that you not let your response to our educational crisis simply evolve. We strongly encourage you to establish a strategic-planning process for your department and to place the responsibility for that planning process on the most qualified, committed faculty you have.

---

[2] As an example of the kind of strategic thinking that must take place at each school, consider how one university has responded. Facing declining accounting enrollments and sensing the need for a broader education, this school eliminated its undergraduate accounting program and now offers only a "12-month Master's of Accountancy program" that admits students who do not have undergraduate accounting degrees. Administrators of the program have had to work hard in recruiting students, but their current number of students is as high as ever and is at capacity. Students admitted generally have no years, or fewer years, of work experience than M.B.A. students and their starting salaries are lower than those of graduating M.B.A. students. The program has proved popular among both liberal arts and undergraduate business students, as well as corporate and professional service recruiters.

Give them the resources they need to complete their work in a timely manner. Set a time horizon that will communicate the urgency of the problem. Quick action is important now.

3. Both of the above-suggested actions apply to individual professors, as well as to departments and programs. All faculty members should use the crisis facing accounting education as an opportunity to evaluate their own situations, and to establish a strategic plan for their careers.[3]

In conducting your strategic planning, there are several steps you could take and questions you should ask. We would recommend that you at least consider the following categories of issues.

Assess the Environment Your Program is Facing

The first step in the strategic-planning process for an accounting department is to assess the environment your programs and faculty face. Here are some questions you should consider.

1. Who have been the primary employers of our students? What will they expect of us in the future, and what are their strengths and weaknesses? Are we happy with these employers or should we seek out different firms to hire our students? How do employers rate our students? What other opportunities might we develop for our students?

2. Where have our students come from and where will they come from in the future? What do our students expect from us? Can we expect student in-flow to continue? If not, what threats do we see? What other areas of recruiting students are available to us?

3. What are the strengths and weaknesses of our faculty today? Do we have excess capacity or do we need more faculty? What do our faculty strengths and weaknesses look like if our student population and/or demographics change?

4. What are the strengths and weaknesses of the business school of which we are a part? What about the university? Do our programs complement and fit in with those of the business school?

5. What resources do we have available? Are those resources at risk if our student population changes? What other avenues for resource development are available to us?

Consider Carefully Every Degree Offered

Second, we would encourage you to examine rigorously all of your educational programs, asking whether they should continue to be offered. You should ask, for example:

1. Should we continue to offer a separate undergraduate program in accounting?

2. Should we combine our accounting degree with a related degree program in strategy, information systems, or finance?

3. Should we offer only an accounting minor?

4. Should we offer a fifth-year or master's program?

5. Should we become a service department to other business-school programs?

6. Should we offer only a concentration within an M.B.A. program?

7. Should we continue offering a Ph.D. program? If so, is it structured correctly?

8. Should we add a new and different kind of program? If so, what should it look like?

These are important questions. Following a one-size-fits-all approach, too many schools try to do too much. Because other schools have a full range of academic programs, many others believe they should as well. It would be far better to do one or two things well. Program alternatives your strategic-planning team might consider include:

---

[3] The findings of this study also have significant implications for the AAA. We urge the Executive Committee to give careful consideration to how it must react to changes in business and needed changes in accounting education in order to continue to provide value-added services to its members.

1. A stand-alone, undergraduate accounting program, designed as a preparatory degree for M.B.A. or other graduate programs, with significantly modified curricula that prepares students for those graduate degrees.

2. A combination undergraduate or graduate degree program with another business discipline.

3. A highly efficient, integrated five-year master's degree in accounting that looks basically like a current M.B.A., but with restructured accounting courses as described below.

4. An accounting minor on top of a broad humanities or social science degree. The three or four accounting courses offered to complete the minor would need to be much different than the typical introductory and intermediate courses we require now.

5. An accounting concentration in a traditional, two-year M.B.A. program, focusing on high-value-chain activities.

6. A Ph.D. program that involves some exposure to pedagogical approaches and curriculum development. An innovative Ph.D. program could involve requiring students to complete joint research with business professionals as well as conduct traditional kinds of empirical, experimental, behavioral, or other research.

Given the changing nature of accounting education and the business world, a combination degree program with a related discipline might be very attractive. One such program would be to follow the lead of the AICPA and IMA and redesign the accounting curriculum so that graduates are consultants/accountants with a strong basis in measurement, but are more broadly equipped to act as business consultants and advisors. Such a program would include some accounting, but would also include more coverage of information systems, economics, and business strategy. Adopting this approach would require the involvement of nonaccounting faculty in the accounting/consultant major or the retraining of existing accounting faculty. The expanded scope of this curriculum would mean a reduction in the amount of time and depth that could be devoted to traditional accounting courses. It might make sense to package this broadened curriculum in a five-year program, as the originators of the 150-hour rule envisioned.

Another strategy would be to develop an accounting/systems degree. Many of our focus-group participants and several of our interviewees suggested that accounting education needs to broaden its understanding of what accounting is and see it as a subset, or extension of, the larger business information system. With a broadly defined "information" perspective of accounting, it is logical that accounting education would evolve as a combination of traditional accounting courses and information systems courses. Again, such a strategy would require a reduced amount of time and depth devoted to traditional accounting and more study of information systems.

A third strategy would be to develop an accounting/finance degree. The vision of accounting as information providers has particular appeal to those who see accounting as useful in corporate decision making and management. Alternatively, accounting can also be seen as a critical element of financial markets. With a financial-market perspective, it may be appropriate to combine accounting and finance into one degree. Such an integrated program would produce a student who has a thorough understanding of the financial-reporting process, how financial reporting affects financial markets, and how financial information can be used and analyzed to make better investment and market decisions.

These are only three of several possible degree combinations available. Whichever strategy is selected, accounting educators will probably have to work hard to eliminate the "silo" mentality and walls that isolate accounting professors and classes from the rest of the business school. Continuing to be an isolated department will not be a wise strategy given the oft-cited need for our graduates to have a broad business background.

For departments and faculty who choose not to broaden their major, abandoning their accounting major altogether and becoming a service provider for other disciplines within the business school might be attractive. Every business graduate must have a fundamental understanding of accounting in the same way that he or she must have a solid grounding in quantitative methods or economics. There is no shame in being a service provider to other degree programs. Such a strategy, however, would require a change in emphasis among the accounting faculty and a much higher degree of integration across the school. It would also probably mean decreased financial resources and a smaller faculty.

Consider Carefully Your Curriculum and Course Content

Third, we would encourage you, in your strategic planning, to rigorously challenge curricula and content from your most introductory accounting course to your most advanced course. Focusing on each course, you would ask questions such as:

1. Is what we are teaching and the level at which we are covering topics really important in the business world today or has technology, globalization, or increased competition dictated that we make substantive changes to our curriculum?

2. Are we teaching important concepts in the most efficient and effective way—that is, are we using the most effective pedagogy in our teaching?

3. Are we partnering sufficiently with related and/or needed courses in other disciplines? Is there an opportunity to eliminate silos in our school?

Each school's faculty must decide for itself how it will answer these questions, based on its own environment. However, based on our acquired understanding of what is occurring, we believe significant changes in curricula and content will be required. Here are a few ideas:

- Introductory accounting might focus less on preparation of financial statements and more on analysis. It might explore the role that accounting plays in capital markets and organizations and explain the structure of the profession. The content might introduce the material that an accountant would need to move into consulting, business advising, and strategic planning.
- The second course might creatively capture managerial topics that focus on using information to make decisions.
- Intermediate accounting should be collapsed into one course, focusing more on analysis and research than on specific standards in detail.

Similarly, why not eliminate separate cost and advanced accounting courses? Why not develop one tax course that focuses on both individual and corporate taxes? Then, think about ways to introduce your students to various industries such as manufacturing, financial services, retail, service, and dot.coms, exposing students to the economic model of companies in the industries, including how they generate profit and are related to other types of companies and to the economy. In addition, find a way to cover risk analysis and control. In particular, we need to renew our commitment to skill development.

The result might be an undergraduate curriculum that covers the following subjects:

1. Accounting and its role in society: The accounting profession

2. Analysis of accounting information: What does accounting information tell us?

3. Using accounting information (financial and nonfinancial) to make decisions

4. Risk analysis and controls

5. Research in financial reporting: where the standards are and how to apply them

6. Using technology in business and decision making (technology as a business aid and the impact of technology on business strategy.)

7. Tax accounting (personal and corporate—income, sales, estate, etc.) and its effect on decision making.

8. Using accounting information in different industries (case-based course using accounting information from different industries, focusing on the nature of those industries as much as the accounting issues involved)

9. Expanded professional services (e.g., personal financial planning, fraud investigations, strategic consulting)

10. A few, but not many, elective courses that allow some specialization

After looking at these subjects, you may say that there is no way all of the topics, grouped together, could be covered in one course. Intermediate, cost, and tax professors, for example, might say that they need several courses to cover their material. Therein lies a major point we are trying to make—we do not need to cover all the traditional material. Students can be exposed to many of these topics at the 25,000-foot level and if we do not get all the topics covered in equal depth, then that's fine. What is important is teaching students how to find answers and how to learn. Frankly, educators have little comparative advantage over practice in delivering high-level technical material. Rather, our competitive advantage is on focusing more on fundamental/foundational material and skill building. This change in orientation will be difficult for many of us who grew up thinking that professors were the preeminent purveyors of knowledge and that students should be captive listeners. Some will question this type of curriculum because it does not include a particular course or courses that they think is important. The curriculum suggested here is only one possible set of courses. The important thing is that each school take a "zero-based" approach to its curriculum—throw away what is no longer needed and try to make its program as value-added as possible.

Consider Carefully the Pedagogy in Every Class

Finally, we would encourage your strategic planning team to challenge rigorously the current pedagogy of every class offered. The team ought to ask questions such as:

1. Do our delivery methods allow students to develop critical skills?

2. Do our delivery methods rely too much on lecture and memorization?

3. Do we use sufficient and appropriate out-of-classroom experiences?

Following the advice of the AECC, it is time that we, in accounting education, move away from our reliance on lecture and move toward teaching approaches that convey critical KSAs—cases that teach dealing with uncertainty and analytical skills, oral and written communication assignments, and quizzes immediately after mini-lectures or videos to teach communication and listening skills. Our pedagogy needs to include some elements of group work to teach leadership and working together, role playing to teach negotiation, technology assignments to teach technology, and larger projects to teach project management. We all need to look for creative ways to involve business professionals in the educational process, and to exploit the potential of out-of-class activities, such as internships, field studies, and service-learning assignments. We should expect our students to do research on the Web and use the wide variety of data services available.

The following diagram illustrates the strategic-planning decisions each program must address:

| What is our environment and what are our resources? Who are our students and employers? | What kinds of programs should we have? Should we form strategic alliances with other programs or disciplines? | What should our course content look like? Which courses should we offer? How should we structure our curriculum? | What kinds of delivery mthods should we use? How do we develop our faculty? How do we measure performance? |

The Need to Invest in Faculty Development

Universities cannot expect faculty who possess outdated skills and knowledge to make the kinds of changes needed today. Accounting faculty studied topics and were educated in ways that are no longer relevant. It is critical that faculty be given the resources to stay up to date, which means that they must develop technologically, globally, and have current and broad business and accounting knowledge. They must be allowed to interact with business professionals and faculty colleagues in other disciplines. Schools that do not invest sufficient resources in faculty development will find that their faculty is unable to make the changes needed today. The result will be programs that continue to shrink in size and diminish in effectiveness.

Faculty must stay engaged, in some form, with the fast-paced changing world of business. Being current means that, in an environment of a shrinking global market, faculty should have global interests and their teaching should include a global perspective. Faculty must have consulting, internship, residency, or other real-world experiences that allow them to understand the kinds and pace of changes taking place.[4] Faculty must be avid readers of other people's research and of current business newspapers and periodicals.

Every program must have a proactive faculty development agenda. Only those programs and faculty that determine how to add value that is distinctive, appreciated by stakeholders, and not easily duplicated by lower-cost competitors will survive. Every program and its faculty must decide what are its competitive advantages and strengths and work hard to maintain those advantages. Faculty development opportunities must be explicitly created and rewarded for programs to remain competitive. While successful faculty members must be in charge of their own faculty development, programs and schools must provide the supportive environment to allow and encourage development to take place.

Concluding Comments

We will conclude this report with one quote from each the four sponsoring organizations about the future of accounting education and accounting careers.

The role of management accountants has evolved from serving internal customers to being a business partner. A business partner is an equal member of the decision-making team. As a business partner, a management accountant has the authority and responsibility to tell an operating executive why particular types of information may or may not be relevant to the business decision at hand and is expected to suggest ways to improve the quality of the decision. —IMA, Counting More, Counting Less, 1999

A fundamental power shift from providers to consumers is taking place in all segments of the economy, including post-secondary education. To remain competitive, institutions need to adopt a customer focus, which will become the key driver in the design and delivery of post-secondary education. Each institution needs to understand the needs of those employer organizations with whom it wishes to place its graduates, the needs of prospective students, including degree requirements, credentialing, and other life-long learning opportunities, and strengths and weaknesses of its competition. Each institution needs to define the unique market niche that will set its programs(s)

---

4   The right kind of consulting experiences, for example, can keep faculty current and bring opportunities to students. While some still argue that consulting, under any circumstance, is inappropriate, consulting is probably the lowest-cost way for a school to keeps its faculty current. Consulting can result in a win-win situation for everyone involved. Students of consulting faculty are more engaged because what they are learning is current and relevant and classes are more interesting and challenging. Professors feel rewarded because they are experiencing research and consulting accomplishments and sharing those accomplishments with their students. Periodic involvement in consulting and other forms of dialogue between academics and professionals enhances the teacher's ability to teach and the researcher's ability to research. Like medicine and law, accounting and business are clinical subjects with the laboratory being the world of business and accounting.

apart from other accounting programs with which it competes. Each institution needs to identify those "high priority" segments of its curricula that will be pivotal in establishing its market niche and then quickly build new curricula in the identified "high priority" areas. Each institution needs to identify new knowledge and skills required to teach the "high priority" segments of its curricula, such as information technology and globalization, and begin to build those skills through faculty development initiatives. —AAA, Report of the Changing Environment Committee, 1998

Many of the traditional, essential skills of CPAs are being replaced by new technologies that are increasing in number and being rapidly developed, often from unexpected sources. Corporations are conducting business in a world of commerce that is global, technological, instantaneous, and increasingly virtual. The leadership they require from both internal and external advisors requires new insights, new skills, and extraordinary agility. CPAs will expand their ability to gather data from a wide variety of sources and increasingly provide valuable strategic interpretations for decision making. —AICPA, CPA Vision, 1999

The accounting profession faces a unique convergence of forces, which creates a critical need to re-examine the educational process. The profession is changing, expanding and, as a result, becoming increasingly complex. Declining enrollments in accounting programs indicate that the profession is becoming less attractive to students....Individuals seeking to be successful in the diverse world of public accounting must be able to use creative problem-solving skills in a consultative process....The current textbook-based, rule-intensive, lecture/problem-solving style should not survive as the primary means of presentation. —Big 8, The White Paper, 1989

These quotes cover a period of 11 years. Yet, the message is the same. Corporate and public accounting firms are working hard to transform themselves into finance professionals and professional services firms. It is now accounting education's turn to transform itself. Failure to do so could be fatal. Seizing the moment to make needed changes could increase our relevance and open new opportunities for accounting education.

APPENDIX

Our Research Methodology

While some of the conclusions made in this report are ours, we tried hard to obtain as much supporting evidence as possible. Our research methodology consisted of four major initiatives. First, we read everything we could find on accounting education. We especially focused on empirical reports and institutional studies such as those prepared for or conducted by the AAA, IMA, and AICPA. We also read many articles on accounting education written by academics. In the bibliography, you will not find references to articles written by accounting educators (unless we quoted directly from their study). These references were purposefully omitted from the bibliography because accounting educators should already be familiar with them and because they can be easily searched.

Second, we interviewed a number of key business, accounting, and education leaders. Throughout the report, you will find quotes from these interviews. These interviews were conducted to help us understand perspectives of those involved in leadership positions and to provide insights that would help interpret the empirical results we found.

Third, we conducted four focus-group sessions with individuals nominated by the four sponsoring organizations. These sessions each included approximately 25–30 educators, corporate accountants, public accountants, and governmental accountants as participants. These focus-group sessions were taped and transcribed. We also participated in the Ross Institute Roundtable at New York University, which essentially served as another focus-group meeting. You will also find quotes from focus-group members in the report.

Focus groups and personal interviews represent qualitative research. We recognize that qualitative research does not allow for the statistical projection of results to the larger population of professionals and educators from which group participants were selected. The sample is too small, and participant selection is not sufficiently random. Further, while every attempt was made to minimize the impact of group dynamics on the expression of individual opinion in the focus groups, the chance remains that some group members either echoed the sentiments of others rather than disagreed or made comments for the sake of effect rather than for reasons of genuine feeling. This does not mean, however, that qualitative research is without value. When qualitative research yields consistent patterns across groups, it is possible to gain valuable information that can be applied to business decisions. Moreover, focus groups provide the emotional depth and breadth of opinion within which statistical data can be interpreted and understood; this depth and breadth can provide a vibrancy absent in quantitative research. Because we used both quantitative and qualitative research methods, we were able to both state generalizable results and understand the depth and vibrancy of the feelings behind those results.

Fourth, we distributed three questionnaire surveys. The actual questionnaires are available from sponsoring organization web sites. Two of these questionnaires were similar and were directed to accounting practitioners and accounting educators. The sponsoring organizations distributed approximately 4,800 questionnaires (1,200 by each organization).[1] Because of the preferences of the sponsoring organizations, these surveys were available to educators and corporate accountants both electronically and in hard copy, but were available only electronically to CPAs. The survey was long, probably accounting for a lower response rate than we desired. We made the early decision that we needed answers to many questions and we were willing to sacrifice a high response rate in order to get more complete information. We sent second requests to nonrespondents. The third survey was a shorter, electronic survey sent to accounting department chairs. This survey was endorsed by both AAA and the Accounting Programs Leadership Group (APLG) leaders.

We met with the Sponsors Task Force three times. The first time, we outlined the project and agreed upon the task to be accomplished. During the second meeting, we received input on our questionnaires and determined focus-group strategy. During the final meeting, we discussed our tentative conclusions and discussed strategy for completing the project and printing the report. Draft reports were read by task-force members and their comments were included in the report where appropriate.

We were under a tight deadline to complete this project. The final charge and approval to conduct the study were given to us in December 1999. The report had to be delivered to the AAA by mid-July 2000 for inclusion in AAA Annual Meeting packets. We tried to be careful not to sacrifice accuracy or thoroughness for the sake of completing the project on time.

---

[1] Because of faulty addresses and other reasons, approximately 4,000 questionnaires were received by potential respondents. The 783 responses received from professionals and educators represents a response rate of approximately 20 percent. The department-chair survey was distributed by the AAA in electronic form only. We received several emails from individuals who said they were no longer serving as department chair, that their school did not have separate accounting departments or separate accounting programs and so the survey wasn't relevant to them, and so forth. We received responses from 134 active department chairs. To ensure that there was no response bias in survey responses, we examined the responses in two separate groups. The first half received was analyzed separately from the last half. Responses to the two sets were nearly identical, suggesting a lack of response bias.

REFERENCES AND RESOURCES

In conducting this study, we had the opportunity to consult with many people. We are grateful for their contributions. We heard from nearly 1,000 individuals who responded to our surveys. We talked with approximately 120 people in four focus groups. We held one-on-one interviews with 20 individuals. We read all the articles and reports of other studies on our subject that we could find. The transcripts we reviewed and the institutional and business publications we consulted are listed below. We also read many academic articles on the subject, but have not referenced them here because our primary audience—accounting educators—should already be familiar with them and because the articles are readily available using normal search devices.

Transcripts of Focus Group Sessions
* Chicago
* New York
* Atlanta
* Los Angeles

Transcripts of Personal Interviews (listed in alphabetical order)
* Fred Allardyce. Chair, Financial Executives Institute; Senior Vice President, American Standard, Inc.
* Jeri Calle. KPMG, Partner-in-Charge, Human Resources—Assurance
* Julie H. Collins. Senior Associate Dean, Kenan-Flagler School of Business, University of North Carolina at Chapel Hill
* Robert K. Elliott. Chair, AICPA Board of Directors; Partner, KPMG
* John Hatfield. Dean, the Merrick School of Business, University of Baltimore
* Paul L. Locatelli. President, Santa Clara University
* Jim Mallak. Executive Vice President and Chief Financial Officer, Textron Automotive Company, Inc.
* Eli Mason. Senior Partner, Mason & Co.; founding Chairman of the National Council of CPA Practitioners
* Patricia McConnell. Senior Managing Director, Bear, Stearns & Co. Inc.
* Bernard J. Milano. President, Beta Alpha Psi; Partner, KPMG
* Frank Minter. President, Institute of Management Accountants
* James H. Naus. Partner, Crowe, Chisek & Company, LLP; former managing partner of the firm
* William F. Ohrt. Vice President and CFO, Dura Automotive Systems, Inc.
* Stephen J. Pickett. Vice President Information Technology, Penske Corporation
* Henry B. Schacht. Director and Senior Advisor, E. M. Warburg, Pincus & Co., LLC; former Chairman and Chief Executive Officer of Lucent Technologies, Inc. and of Cummins Engine Company, Inc.
* William G. Shenkir. Farrish Professor of Free Enterprise, the McIntire School of Commerce, University of Virginia; former Dean of the School

- Jerry D. Sullivan. Executive Director, the Public Oversight Board
- Robert J. Swieringa. Lindsmith Dean, the Johnson Graduate School of Management, Cornell University
- Judy Tsui. Professor and Department Chair, City University of Hong Kong
- Lynn E. Turner. Chief Accountant, U.S. Securities and Exchange Commission

Institutional and Business Articles and Studies

- Accounting Education Change Commission (AECC). 1990. Objectives of education for accountants: Position statement number one. *Issues in Accounting Education* (Fall): 307–312.
- American Accounting Association (AAA), Committee on the Future Structure, Content, and Scope of Accounting Education (The Bedford Committee). 1986. Future accounting education: Preparing for the expanding profession. *Issues in Accounting Education* (Spring): 168–195.
- ————, Report of the Changing Environment Committee. 1998. *The Future Viability of Accounting Education*. Sarasota, FL: AAA.
- American Assembly of Collegiate Schools of Business (AACSB). 1995–1996. *A Report of the AACSB Faculty Leadership Task Force*. St Louis, MO: AACSB.
- ————. 1999. Brand name B-schools partnering with start-ups for revenue and research. *Newsline* (Fall): 1–9.
- ————. 2000. Hurr-e up: B-schools striving to get e-business courses and resources up to speed. *Newsline* (Winter): 1–11.
- American Institute of Certified Public Accountants (AICPA), The AICPA Special Committee on Financial Reporting. 1994. *Improving Business Reporting—A Customer Focus: Meeting the Information Needs of Investors and Creditors*. New York, NY: AICPA.
- ————, CPA Vision Project: Focus on the Horizon. 1998. *Executive Summary and CPA Vision Project Focus Groups: Public Practice, Industry, and Government CPAs; also an Addendum: Student Focus Groups*. New York, NY: AICPA.
- ————. 1997. *Supply of Accounting Graduates and the Demand for Public Accounting Recruits*. New York, NY: AICPA.
- ————. 1998. CPA vision project identifies top five issues for profession. *The CPA Letter* (April): 1, 12.
- ————. 1998. 150-hour education requirement. AICPA web site: http://www.aicpa.org/members/div/career/150bkg.htm.
- Asahi Evening News. 2000. Universities no longer an ivory tower. (February 10).
- Baker, Cunningham, Kimmel, and Venable. 1995. *Critical Thinking*. Edited by Pincus. St. Louis, MO: Federation of Schools of Accountancy.
- Bartlett, T. 2000. The hottest campus on the Internet. *Business Week* (January 14): online.
- Berton, L. 1994. College courses on accounting get poor grade. *Wall Street Journal* (August 12): B1.
- Birkett, W., M. Barbera, B. Leithhead, M. Lower, and P. Roebuck. 1999. *The Future of Internal Auditing: A Delphi Study*. Six volumes. Altamonte Springs, FL: The Institute of Internal Auditors Research Foundation.
- Boyer, E. 1990. *Scholarship Reconsidered*. Princeton, NJ: The Carnegie Foundation for the Advancement of Teaching.
- Brackner, J. W. 2000. *Suggested Framework for Accounting Curriculum to Begin the 21st Century*. Montvale, NJ: IMA.
- Brown, D. G. 1999. *Always in Touch: A Practical Guide to Ubiquitous Computing*. Winston-Salem, NC: Wake Forest University Press.

- Buckman, R. 2000. What price a BMW? At Stanford it may cost only a resume. *Wall Street Journal* (May 19): A1.
- *Business Week.* 2000. Where have all the accountants gone? (March 27): 203–204.
- Byrne, J. A. 2000. Virtual B schools. *Business Week* (January 14): online.
- Cargille, Engstrom, Jeffery, and Lavin. 1996. *Ethics.* Edited by Cunningham. St. Louis, MO: Federation of Schools of Accountancy.
- Cottel, Drews-Bryan, and McKenzie. 1995. *Cooperative Learning.* Edited by Pincus. St. Louis, MO: Federation of Schools of Accountancy.
- *The Economist.* 1999. Strength in numbers. (November 20): 86.
- Edmonds, Olds, Ravenscroft, and Rusth. 1996. *Testing.* Edited by Cunningham. St. Louis, MO: Federation of Schools of Accountancy.
- Elliott, R. K. 1999. Steering a course for the future. Incoming AICPA chairman remarks, Seattle, WA, October 19.
- Ernst & Young LLP. 1994. *The Challenge of Pervasive Change: Business Education in the Year 2000.* New York, NY: Ernst & Young.
- Fleming, P. D. 1999. Steering a course for the future. *Journal of Accountancy* (November): 35–39.
- Grimes, A. 2000. A matter of degree. *Wall Street Journal* (July 17): R29.
- Hardin, J. R, D. O'Bryan, and J. J. Quirin. 2000. Accounting versus engineering, law and medicine: Perceptions of influential high school teachers. *Advances in Accounting* (17): 205–220.
- Hargadon, J. 2000. Accounting education: The challenges ahead. PICPA Special Insert, Special Millennium Insert. AICPA. New York, NY.
- Independence Standards Board (ISB). 1999. *Report to the Independence Standards Board: Research into Perceptions of Auditor Independence and Objectivity.* New York, NY: ISB.
- Institute of Internal Auditors (IIA). 1999. *A Vision for the Future: Professional Practice Framework for Internal Auditors.* Report of the Guidance Task Force to the IIA's Board of Directors. Altamonte Springs, FL: IIA.
- Institute of Management Accountants (IMA). 1994. *What Corporate America Wants in Entry-Level Accountants.* Executive summary (with the Financial Executives Institute). Montvale, NJ: IMA.
- ———. 1996. *The Practice Analysis of Management Accounting: Results of Research.* Montvale, NJ: IMA.
- ———. 1999. *Counting More, Counting Less: Transformations in the Management Accounting Profession.* Montvale, NJ: IMA.
- ———. 1999. Major shift away from traditional accounting functions revealed in largest continuing analysis of management accounting. *IMA Focus* (September-November): 1–2.
- ———. 1999. What corporate accountants do! Presentation by C. S. Kulesza, K. Russell, and G. Sundem to the 1999 American Accounting Association Annual Meeting, San Diego, CA.
- International Federation of Accountants (IFA). 2000. *Quality Issues for Internet and Distributed Learning in Accounting Education.* New York, NY: IFA.
- King, J. 2000. Techno MBAs pay off. *Computer World* (January 14): online.
- Melancon, B. 1998. The changing strategy for the profession, the CPA and the AICPA: What this means for the education community. *Accounting Horizons* (December): 397–408.
- Milano, B. 1999. Letter to accounting professors re: Changes in the structure of Beta Alpha Psi. New York, NY.
- Morreale, J., and C. Licata. 1997. *Post Tenure Review: A Guide Book for Academic Administrators of Colleges and Schools of Business.* St. Louis, MO: AACSB.

- *Perspectives on Education: Capabilities for Success in the Accounting Profession* (The White Paper). 1989. Arthur Andersen & Co., Arthur Young, Coopers & Lybrand, Deloitte Haskins & Sells, Ernst & Whinney, Peat Marwick Main & Co., Price Waterhouse, and Touche Ross. New York, NY.
- Petersen, M. 1999. Shortage of accounting students raises concerns on audit quality. *New York Times* (February 19): A1, C3–4.
- Pethley and Fremgen. 1999. What's in a name change? *Journal of Accountancy* (August): 71–74.
- Public Oversight Board (POB). 1999. Transcripts of the hearings before the Audit Effectiveness Task Force. Stamford, CT: POB.
- Rebele, Stout, Saunders, and O'Conner. 1996. *Communication*. Edited by Cunningham. St. Louis, MO: Federation of Schools of Accountancy.
- Rowley, D., H. Lujan, and M. Dolence. 1998. *Strategic Choices for the Academy: How Life Long Learning Will Recreate Higher Education.* San Francisco, CA: Jossey-Bass Publishers.
- Russell, K., and H. Bell. 1998. *Financial Professionals in the Corporate World: Best Practice.* Videos. Montvale, NJ: IMA.
- ———, and Berlin, S. 1999. Accounting education: A position statement for the new millennium. *Management Accounting Quarterly* (Fall): 35–42.
- ———, G. Siegel, and C. S. Kulesza. 1999. Counting more, counting less. *Strategic Finance* (September): 39–44.
- Siegel, G., and C. S. Kulesza. 1996. The coming changes in management accounting education. *Management Accounting* (January): 43–47.
- Sundem, G. L. 1999. *The Accounting Education Change Commission: Its History and Impact.* Sarasota, FL: AAA.
- Weber, T. E. 2000. Allen is wooing elite colleges to teach online. *Wall Street Journal* (July 28): B1.
- Wilkerson, J. 2000. *A Report on Undergraduate Business Program Quality Factors.* Wayne Calloway School of Business and Accountancy. Wake Forest University, Winston-Salem, NC.
- Winter, G. 2000. In the boom, desperately seeking bean counters. *New York Times* (June 28): 11.

Audio-Visual Materials
- American Accounting Association/AICPA Faculty Development Alliance. 2000. *Technology Accounting Education Practice: A Showcase of Successful Ideas.* CD-ROM. Sarasota, FL.
- American Accounting Association, The Accounting Education Change Commission. 1999. *Change in Accounting Education: Output from the Accounting Education Change Commission.* CD-ROM. Sarasota, FL.
- AICPA. 1997. *Report of the Special Committee on Assurances Services.* CD-ROM. New York, NY.
- ———. 1999. *The CPA Vision: 2001 and Beyond.* The future is in your hands. CD-ROM. New York, NY.
- ———. 2000. Top technologies 2000: Highlights. Video. New York, NY.
- ———. 2000. XFRML. EXtensible Financial Reporting Markup Language. Exposure draft on web site: http://www.xbrl.org.
- The Ross Institute, The Stern School, New York University. 2000. *The Demand for and Supply of Accounting Professionals in the Year 2000 and Beyond.* Ross Institute Roundtable, April 3. Video. New York, NY.